ALTERNATIVE WORK SCHEDULES

Part 2: Permanent Part-Time Employment

Part 3: The Compressed Workweek

an AMA survey report

Stanley D. Nollen
Virginia H. Martin

A DIVISION OF AMERICAN MANAGEMENT ASSOCIATIONS

Stanley D. Nollen is an assistant professor in the School of Business Administration at Georgetown University. Alternative work schedules are one of his chief research interests. He has done research on permanent part-time employment for the U.S. Department of Labor and has made presentations to a variety of groups of business people and educators. His book (with Brenda Eddy and Virginia Martin), *Part-Time Employment: The Manager's Perspective,* will be published by Praeger in their Special Studies Series in 1978. He also does research in industrial education and training and has written articles on paid educational leave of absence for workers and on lifelong learning. In the School of Business Administration, he teaches Managerial Economics and Social Responsibilities of Business. He received his M.B.A. degree in 1970 and his Ph.D. in 1974, both from the University of Chicago.

Virginia Hider Martin was one of the United States' earliest proponents of flexitime. Her study of the experience of public and private sector organizations with flexible working hours, *Hours of Work When Workers Can Choose,* was published in 1975. An independent organizational development consultant in Alexandria, Virginia, she is currently associated with the U.S. Civil Service Commission. She was a founder of the National Council For Alternative Work Patterns and chaired the program committee for the first National Conference on Alternative Work Schedules. She is a member of the American Society for Training and Development and the Industrial Relations Research Association, and co-author with Stanley Nollen and Brenda Eddy of a book on part-time employment that is to be published by Praeger in 1978.

© 1978 AMACOM
A division of American Management Associations, New York. All rights reserved. Printed in the United States of America.

This Survey Report has been distributed to all members enrolled in the American Management Associations. Extra copies are available at $7.50 a copy for AMA members, $10.00 a copy for nonmembers.

First Printing

Library of Congress Cataloging in Publication Data

Nollen, Stanley D.
    Permanent part-time employment.

    (Their Alternative work schedules ; v. 2-3)
(An AMA survey report)
    Includes bibliographies.
    1. Part-time employment--United States.
2. Four-day week--United States. I. Martin,
Virginia Hider, joint author. II. Nollen,
Stanley D. The compressed workweek. 1978.
III. Title. IV. Series: American Management
Association. An AMA survey report.
HD5124.N64 vol. 2-3 [HD5110.2.U5] 331.2'572'0973s
ISBN 0-8144-3134-8   [331.2'572'0973] 78-17323

Contents

Introduction

Interest in alternative work schedules is high and rising—especially among management and labor groups. In addition, some professional associations and research institutes are calling for more study and development of such schedules. A number of national and regional conferences on the topic for business, labor, government, and academic people have been held in the last three years. These schedules are being supported by several advocacy groups—including those representing the interests of women, retirees, the handicapped, and environmentalists. Media attention is growing, including that of the business press. Several pieces of legislation on alternative work schedules are pending in the U.S. Congress, and some states have already enacted such legislation. Employers themselves, in both private and public sectors, have begun experiments with alternative work schedules; many such schedules are currently in use.

What Are Alternative Work Schedules?

The term *alternative work schedules* encompasses all variations of the standard work schedule: that is, a workday from 8:00 or 9:00 a.m. to 5:00 p.m., for seven or eight hours a day, five days a week. Chief among such systems are:

- *Flexible Working Hours (Flexitime)*. Employees may vary their starting and stopping time within limits, but work the contracted number of hours in a specified time period (day, week, or month).
- *Compressed Workweek*. The usual number of weekly full-time hours is compressed into fewer than five days.
- *Permanent Part-Time Employment*. Regular voluntary employment (not temporary or casual) is carried out during working hours distinctly shorter than normal.

Another alternative work pattern is staggered hours, in which some employees are scheduled to arrive and depart earlier (7:30 a.m. to 4:30 p.m., for example) than others (who may, for example, arrive at 8:30 a.m. and leave at 5:30 p.m.). If the staggered hours are employee-chosen, this system is considered a restricted form of flexitime.

The task system is another alternative work schedule—one in which a task or specified quantity of work is assigned to be completed within a given time period. In practice, a day's work is usually assigned and employees are free to leave when it is finished. Few examples of this system, also known as earned time, exist—though it is used for sanitation workers and meter readers in some cities.

Part 1 of this survey report, recently published, discussed flexitime results. (See Nollen, Stanley and Martin, Virginia, *Alternative Work Schedules, Part 1: Flexitime*, New York, AMACOM—a division of American Management Associations.) Here, Parts 2 and 3 discuss results of the research on permanent part-time employment and the compressed workweek. (Neither staggered hours nor the task system was researched.)

Alternative Work Schedules in an Industrial Relations Context

Alternative work schedules are new developments in industrial relations. They pose new ideas for employment policies of organizations. Flexitime began in Germany in 1967 and spread rapidly throughout Europe, but received little attention in the U.S. until 1972. Compressed workweeks developed in the U.S. beginning in the late 1960s, but have never been important in Europe. Although part-time employment has been known and practiced for many years, interest in *permanent* part-time employment (not temporary or casual) increased both in Europe and the U.S. in the 1960s. Part-time employment has always been more prevalent in the U.S. than in Europe. However, the tight labor market that persisted in Europe into the 1960s stimulated interest in part-time employment there as a means of increasing the labor supply.

Alternative work schedules are basically human resources development strategies. The best interests of workers are foremost in all of them. But alternative work schedules also offer benefits to employers and they serve the public interest as well.

The fundamental feature of flexible working hours and permanent part-time employment for workers is that they offer new freedom of choice and autonomy. They contribute to the quality and dignity of working life, offering workers more control over their working time and the ability to accommodate personal and family needs as well as work needs. They permit workers to be treated as responsible adults, and they may increase job satisfaction. Compressed workweeks offer workers longer usable blocks of free time. And, though yet largely unrealized, alternative work schedules may also facilitate lifelong learning since the new time management possibilities involved permit adult workers to take advantage of educational opportunities.

For employers, the benefits of alternative work schedules lie in the potentially higher productivity to be gained from more satisfied and more highly motivated workers, and the prospect of using the alternative schedules feature of jobs to attract people with high-level capabilities. Moreover, alternative work schedules give new flexibility to employers as well as to workers. They expand the range of options for solving problems of work scheduling or meeting customer service needs. Another attractive feature for employers is that implementing such schedules costs very little in visible dollars and cents. But they do present a management challenge and, at least initially, require new management thinking and additional management inputs.

Two major sets of social benefits may flow from the use of alternative work schedules. First, a variety of public services and facilities can be provided more efficiently. Chief among these are more evenly distributed commuting traffic flows, demands for public transportation (with potentially reduced energy consumption), and usage of recreational facilities. Second, employment opportunities for several groups of people are improved, particularly women, men who wish a more balanced work and home life, the handicapped, and the aging.

How widely are permanent part-time and compressed workweeks used? Who is using them? What experiences do employers have with them? What are the good results they actually yield to the organization? What problems do they bring? How does management respond? These are major questions for managers for which better answers are needed. But before we report on our survey results here, a stocktaking is in order. What do we already know about alternative work schedules? What key issues require new information?

The State of Current Knowledge

Some data are available on the extent to which permanent part-time employment and compressed workweeks are used in the U.S. They show that a quite small proportion of the labor force is currently working a compressed workweek, that a surprisingly large proportion is working at part-time jobs, and that both are very unevenly distributed across industries and occupations.

Permanent Part-Time Employment

Part-time employment, overall is quite common. In 1976, 21.5 percent of all employed persons worked part-time (less than 35 hours per week), but not all of these were *permanent* part-time workers. This figure is not precisely known, but about 8 percent of all workers had part-time jobs year round (48 or more weeks per year); this can be taken as a minimum estimate of permanent part-time employment (U.S. Bureau of Labor Statistics, 1977). The average hours worked per week by part-time employees is 18. Part-time employment is more common among women workers—accounting for a third of their numbers—than it is for men, one-eighth of whom work part-time. And it is more common among young and old workers than it is among middle-aged workers. There has been a gradual increase in part-time employment over time—up one-third as a proportion of all employment since the early 1950s. But this increase has been concentrated in temporary rather than permanent part-time employment.

Part-time employment, like compressed workweeks, is unevenly distributed across industries and occupations. It is most common in the tertiary sector—that is, in wholesale and retail trade and in service industries where, respectively, 24.1 and 21.9 percent of all workers are voluntary part-timers—and least common in manufacturing, where only 4.3 percent of employment is voluntary part-time (U.S. Bureau of Labor Statistics, 1977). In many organizations that have part-time workers, they constitute a small share of the workforce—perhaps 5 percent (Bureau of National Affairs, 1974).

Occupations in which part-time people are concentrated are mainly routine and low-skill occupations, such as service workers (40 percent part-timers), sales workers (34.6 percent), clerical workers (25.1 percent), and laborers (28.4 percent). They are least represented among managers (6.2 percent).

There have been a few previous studies of employers' experiences with part-time employment—some case studies (for example: Control Data, 1974; Catalyst, 1971; Howell and Ginsburg, 1971; and van der Does de Willebois, 1967) and some surveys (for example: Nollen, Eddy, and Martin, 1978; Martin, 1975; Weinstein, 1975; Bureau of National Affairs, 1974; Owen, 1978; McCarthy, 1977; Pryves, 1974; and Schwartz, 1964). From these studies, a few findings about part-time employment from the manager's perspective can be reported.

Chief among the advantages of permanent part-time employment reported in previous studies is that it helps managers solve work scheduling problems (for example, cyclical demands for services, evening or weekend hours, or workloads too large or too small for full-time staffing)—and thus obviously saves labor costs. But it may also introduce some scheduling problems of its own, since part-time workers are not always present.

Another aspect of part-time employment that is sometimes an advantage and sometimes a disadvantage is the nature of labor supply. In some labor markets and for some occupations, an abundance of superior workers is available, so part-time recruiting is easy; in other labor markets, and for other occupations, however, employers report difficulty in finding part-time workers. As with flexitime, productivity and absenteeism are apparently better in many cases for part-time employees than for their full-time counterparts.

The problems with permanent part-time employment, according to previous reports from employers, appear to be that supervision is sometimes made more difficult (perhaps because of the discontinuity introduced) and that some administrative costs, such as recordkeeping, are higher (when part-time employment means more workers or special records). Turnover is frequently feared to be worse for part-time than for full-time employees, but the empirical studies to date do not verify that fear. Similarly, fringe benefits could potentially be higher for part-time employees if all benefits were paid in full—but in practice, employers appear to withhold some fringe benefits so that their costs are not excessive.

Compressed Workweeks

There is quite a low level of use of compressed workweeks. In 1976, 2.1 percent of all full-time nonfarm wage and salary workers (1,270,000 people) were working fewer than five days a week. Growth in compressed workweeks was rapid, beginning from almost no use in 1971 (.1 percent of all workers) to 1.7 percent in 1973 and 2.2 percent by 1975 (U.S. Bureau of Labor Statistics, 1977). But the growth appears to have peaked out, with many organizations returning to the five-day week. (Estimates of failure rates range from 10 to 50 percent. See Haldi, forthcoming.) Most compressed workweeks (60 percent) are 4-day weeks, but 3-day and 4½-day weeks have gained in popularity. People on compressed workweeks are less likely to work 40 hours a week than are five-day people—and also more likely to work either 35 to 39 hours, or more than 40 hours.

Compressed workweeks are used more heavily in some industries than in others. For example, 12.4 percent of full-time wage and salary workers in local public administration were on compressed workweeks—while only .5 percent in mining, .6 percent in federal and state public administration, and 1.6 percent in manufacturing and trade industries worked less than five days a week. Similarly, some occupations have more people on compressed workweeks than do others. For example, compressed workweeks are scarce among managers (.8 percent) and professionals (1.4 percent), but more common among service workers (6.1 percent) and transport equipment operatives (4.8 percent).

A variety of benefits have been claimed for compressed workweeks, both for employers and for workers. Correspondingly, a number of disadvantages have been suggested. Some of these supposed good points and bad points have been evaluated in a few case studies (see, for example, Nord and Costigan, 1973; Mathis, 1972; Swierczewski, 1972; Goodale and Aagard, 1974; Swerdloff, 1976; Steele, 1974; and Ivancevich, 1974) and a few surveys have been made (for example: Wheeler, Gurman, and Tarnowieski, 1972; Poor, 1970; Bureau of National Affairs, 1972; Wilson, 1973; Davis, 1973; Tellier, 1974; Weinstein, 1975; U.S. Comptroller General, 1976; and Hartman and Weaver, 1977).

From these studies, as well as from theoretical expectations, a number of statements about the advantages and disadvantages of compressed workweeks can be tentatively offered.

Previous reports indicate that each of the trio—turnover, absenteeism, and tardiness—is likely to be reduced under a compressed workweek, along with an increase in morale and easier recruiting. The productivity results, however, are in question. On the one hand, there are fewer start-ups and shutdowns under a 4-day than a 5-day workweek, there may in some cases be better utilization of capital equipment, and operating costs may be decreased if a plant or office is not open the fifth day. On the other hand, some complaints of worker fatigue resulting from longer days have been noted—so under compressed workweeks, both positive and negative forces act on productivity. Overtime may need to be paid for hours worked beyond eight in a day.

Another disadvantage of compressed workweeks, reported in other studies, is the problem some employees have in managing their personal commitments (such as evening meetings or the pick-up of children from daycare centers), which works to offset recruiting and turnover advantages. For the employer, work scheduling and communication are often reported to be complicated, especially when some units are on compressed workweeks and others are not. Customer service or vendor service may be worsened if the office or plant is closed on a regular workday.

Research Objectives and Methods

There are several questions about the use of permanent part-time employment and compressed workweeks for which there are now no satisfactory answers. The objective of this study is to provide some answers to these questions. The key questions are:

1. What kinds of jobs and work settings are suited to the use of these alternative work schedules? Who are the users and the non-users? Do these alternative work schedules fit some industries and operating schedules better than others? Are they more common in large or in small firms?

2. How do these alternative work schedules affect the whole range of possible business results—from productivity to public relations, from employee morale to management problems, from direct labor costs to overhead costs? Are there hard data to document these results?

3. What explains the good results and the bad results of these alternative work schedules? What characteristics of organizations and their management are likely to improve the results? Which of the various models of compressed workweeks and permanent part-time employment give the best results?

4. How are these alternative work schedules implemented? What management steps are taken? What changes are made elsewhere in the organization? What problems are encountered? How are they solved?

5. What role do labor unions play in the use of permanent part-time employment and

compressed workweeks? Under what conditions do they assist or oppose them? How many workers on these alternative work schedules are union members?

6. For compressed workweeks in particular: How do the business results change with longer experience? Do good results hold up over time—or do they spring from a kind of Hawthorne effect and thus die off quickly? Do negative aspects persist or can

they be overcome with more experience?

7. Also for compressed workweeks: How many employers have discontinued the use of compressed workweeks and converted back to a standard 5-day week? Why have they done so? What are the future prospects for compressed workweeks?

8. For permanent part-time employment: What kind of part-time employment models are most often used—part-day/full-week or

Exhibit 1. Description of the sample: Industry, sector, and size of organization.

Characteristic	Compressed Workweek		Permanent Part-Time Employment	
	Number	Percent	Number	Percent
Industry				
Construction	12	7%	12	2%
Manufacturing	69	38	180	37
Transportation, communication, and utilities	8	4	45	9
Wholesale and retail trade	9	5	31	6
Finance, insurance, and real estate	40	22	112	23
Services	15	8	60	12
Government	7	4	32	7
Diversified	15	8	15	3
Other	5	3	5	1
Totals	180	99%	492	100%
Sector				
Private	144	92%	433	90%
(profit)	(133)	(85)	(388)	(81)
(nonprofit)	(11)	(7)	(45)	(9)
Public (federal, state, and local)	12	8	46	10
Totals	156	100%	479	100%
Size of Organization				
Number of employees				
less than 100	17	11%	24	5%
100–499	47	30	120	25
500–1000	17	11	82	17
more than 1,000	75	48	255	53
Totals	156	100%	479	100%
Annual sales or budget				
less than $25 million	53	37%	130	29%
$25 to $99 million	26	18	112	25
$100 to $999 million	36	25	133	30
more than $1 billion	28	20	73	16
Totals	143	100%	448	100%

Note: Sample size totals are different in each part of this exhibit because not all respondents answered all questions.

full-day/part-week? How much job sharing is there? How many part-time minishifts are there? How are fringe benefits handled?

Previous survey research on compressed workweeks and permanent part-time employment is scarce. Studies by Martin (1975), Weinstein (1975) and Nollen, Eddy, and Martin (1978) formed an empirical basis for this research, but they were limited by small sample sizes (n = 66 users of compressed workweeks and n = 45 users of part-time employment in Martin, n = 63 users of compressed workweeks in Weinstein—she did not study part-time employment—and n = 68 users of permanent part-time employment in Nollen, Eddy, and Martin). A large survey by Wheeler, Gurman, and Tarnowieski (1972) on compressed workweeks (n = 1,056 total respondents and 145 users of compressed workweeks) and a smaller survey by the Bureau of National Affairs, 1972 (n = 81) are currently quite out of date since their data refer to 1971, when compressed workweeks were just becoming popular. Although there are some more recent surveys, they have very small sample sizes—n = 15 to 25— or have limited data, as in Hartman and Weaver.

By contrast, the larger number of respondents obtained in this study permits more reliable answers, better projections, and better analysis of reasons for certain results. The existence of these previous surveys permits some comparisons to be made of employers' experiences—comparisons that provide the longer run view of the results and problems involved that employers contemplating alternative work schedules might expect.

The analysis in the report to follow is based on 805 usable returned mail questionnaires (28 percent) from a survey of 2,889 organizations conducted in June and July 1977 on alternative work schedules. There were 156 responses from users of compressed workweeks and 481 responses from users of permanent part-time employment. The balance of responses were from users of flexitime who did not also use another alternative work schedule (for discussion of flexitime results, see Part 1 of this Survey Report, previously published by Nollen and Martin, 1978).*

Two populations were sampled: (1) 2,091 organizations in which a senior manager (president, vice-president for human resources, or personnel director, for example) was a customer of the American Management Associations in 1975-77, by virtue of either seminar attendance or publication purchase and (2) 798 suspected users of one or more alternative work schedules. The latter sample was necessary to provide a large enough number of users from which to learn experiences. A substantial number of responses was secured for each of several major industry and size-of-firm groups, in both public and private sectors. A variety of operating schedules and work technologies are represented, and both organizations with heavy and light labor union membership and female employment are in the sample (see Exhibit 1).

---

*To adjust for possible bias in survey results caused by nonresponse, telephone mini-interviews were conducted among nonrespondents to determine whether their answers to a few key effects of flexitime on the organization were the same as those provided by respondents. They were similar, so response bias for flexitime results is small. Separate determinations of response bias for results for compressed workweeks and part-time employment, however, were not made.

Part 2: Permanent Part-Time Employment

1
Highlights and Conclusions

Part-time employment has been used by many employers for a long time. But permanent part-time employment—which is regular and voluntary, not intermittent or casual—is now attracting increased interest as an element of an organization's employment policy. In addition to satisfying personal needs for many people, it may solve some business problems. It can also bring some problems that require management solutions.

How Much Part-Time Employment Is There?

About 22 percent of all employed people in the U.S. are part-time (all workers putting in less than 35 hours a week on the average, including temporaries), according to the U.S. Bureau of Labor Statistics. This figure is up a third from a generation ago.

Part-time employment is especially common among employed women, accounting for a third of their numbers, whereas just an eighth of all men workers are part-timers. Both young and old people are also especially likely to be working part-time.

There is relatively little part-time employment in manufacturing firms (only 4.3 percent of manufacturing workers are part-time), and among managers (only 6.2 percent work part time). Instead, part-time employment is concentrated in trade and service industries, and among service, sales, and clerical workers.

Permanent part-time workers, on the other hand—those who work part-time year round (48 or more weeks)—constitute about 8 percent of the labor force.

Part-Time Employment Models

There are several ways to schedule permanent part-time workers. The most common part-time employment model is part-day employment. It was used by three-quarters of all the respondents in this survey who had part-time workers. Part-week or part-month employment was less common. The part-time minishift and job sharing were each found among just under a quarter of all users.

Where Is Part-Time Employment Used? Where Is It Not Used?

Three characteristics of organizations encourage the use of permanent part-time employment: production of services rather than goods, cyclic demand for output (peak midday business, for example, as in banks), and extended hours of operation (evening hours, for example, as in department stores).

Organizations that have permanent part-time workers typically have only a relatively small number of them—less than 5 percent of their workforce in a majority of cases. Furthermore, such part-time employment is usually found in certain jobs and work units, especially clerical and office jobs, instead of being widely spread throughout the organization.

Labor unions are a deterrent to part-time employment. Unionized companies are less likely to use part-time employees and, if they do, they are less likely to include union members as part-time workers. Only one user out of ten had as much as 10 percent of its part-time workers in a union. Many managers believe that collective bargaining agreements effectively bar part-time employment, or that unions oppose it and seek to limit it to particular situations.

Experiences with Permanent Part-Time Employment

Permanent part-time employment has several important effects on the organizations that use it. Good effects reported by respondents (from all major industries) indicate that it:
- Reduces labor costs:
  Saves overtime payments (for 69 percent of users).
  Reduces straight wage costs (for 58 percent of users).
  Reduces unit labor costs (for 52 percent of users).
- Improves job performance:
  Increases productivity (for three users out of five).
  Reduces fatigue (for three users out of five).
  Reduces absenteeism (for almost half the users).

There are also a few negative effects that pose challenges to management. For example, for roughly one in every three users, part-time employment:
- Increases the difficulty of internal communication.
- Makes the manager's job harder.
- Increases personnel administration costs.
- Increases training costs.

Other management aspects of permanent part-time employment reflect mixed results; they are sometimes advantages and sometimes disadvantages, depending on the user. For example:
- Coverage of work situations is better for 56

percent of the users but worse for 22 percent.
- Work scheduling and employee scheduling are better for a third of the users, worse for a third, and unchanged for a third.
- Fringe benefit costs are lower for 57 percent of the users (because they do not pay all benefits to part-time workers) but higher for 19 percent (because some fringe benefits are proportionately more expensive for part-time workers).

A large majority of these reports are based on managers' opinions rather than on hard numerical data from in-house surveys or studies.

What Do Non-Users Think?

Organizations that do not use permanent part-time employment are more pessimistic about its management aspects than users are. Nearly three-quarters of the non-users believe the difficulty of the management job will be increased and a majority foresee problems with scheduling and coverage. Two-thirds think personnel administration costs and training would be raised by part-time employment. But, on balance, non-users are positive about both savings in labor costs and the job performance of permanent part-time workers.

Some but not all of these differences between users and non-users arise from misperceptions on the part of non-users, so there are some opportunities for expanded use of permanent part-time employment—given better information and education.

Implementation

A dominant reason for using part-time employment is to solve a scheduling problem: Three quarters of all users offered this reason, among others. Secondarily, advantages with respect to labor supply and worker quality were cited. Productivity and labor cost reasons were not directly mentioned very often, indicating that part-time employment is thought of as a solution to a management problem and is not reckoned strictly in terms of economic benefit/cost.

As it is currently practiced, implementation of permanent part-time employment is a simple matter. Only two implementation steps are often taken: Meetings are held with managers and supervisors, and it is instituted first on a trial basis by about 40 percent of all users. Business results from part-time employment are seldom audited; only 6 percent of the responding users did so.

Problems with Permanent Part-Time Employment

Although scheduling problems in the organization were the greatest single reason reported for using permanent part-time employment, some respondents reported scheduling problems with part-time employment itself—lack of coverage, lack of continuity, difficult communication, complicated supervision, and problems of meshing the part-time worker's schedule with the workplace schedule.

Fringe benefits were also cited as a problem by some users—and, in fact, as a reason for not using part-time employment by some non-users. In addition, non-users feared that part-timers would lack commitment, dedication, and loyalty —but, in the experience of users, this was not a problem.

Fringe Benefits

Fringe benefits are a controversial issue in part-time employment. They can—but need not and seldom do—cost more for part-time than for full-time workers. However, this issue deters some organizations from using it and in any event requires careful management attention. According to respondents, most (80 percent) permanent part-time workers get vacation leave. Just over half get sick leave, life and health insurance, and pension benefits. In most cases these benefits are prorated on the basis of hours worked or earnings, and sometimes eligibility conditions are set up (for example, fringe benefits available only to employees who work half the regular time or more). The greatest concern that managers of permanent part-time employment have about fringe benefits is ERISA, which regulates pension plans. ERISA requires that all employees who work 1,000 hours or more a year (about half time) must be treated alike and included in a pension plan if there is one.

2
How and Where Permanent Part-Time Employment Is Used

Permanent part-time employment—regular, voluntary employment carried out during working hours distinctly shorter than normal—needs to be distinguished from other varieties of part-time employment. It is *not* temporary employment, which means employment of fixed duration, either part-time or full-time (seasonal employment is one example, and another is the kind of employment provided by temporary help services). Nor is it intermittent employment—the kind in which the availability or duration of work is unpredictable. Neither is it short hours or involuntary part-time employment, in which shorter-than-normal weeks are worked because of an economic downturn. Instead, permanent part-time employment is stable and ongoing and can constitute career employment.

Permanent part-time employment can be used in a variety of ways and places. What kinds of models are actually used? What kinds of organizations use it? What kinds of jobs do permanent part-time employees do?

Permanent Part-Time Employment Models

Permanent part-time employment may be either (1) part-day employment or (2) full-day, but part-week or part-month. Part-day employment is more common. It was found in three-quarters of the responding organizations that use permanent part-time employment, while the full-day but part-week or part-month alternative was found among just under half the users (see Exhibit 2).

Two different part-time options are the part-time minishift and job sharing. In the case of the minishift, part-time employees work a short shift (perhaps four or five hours) before or after a regularly scheduled full time shift; for example, part-time workers arrive at 5:00 p.m. (as full-time employees are leaving) and work until 10:00 p.m.

The part-time minishift allows increased utilization of existing office or plant space and equipment to get work done that requires more than eight hours, but less than 16 hours, to complete. It may also avoid the need to schedule overtime for full-time day workers if certain departments would otherwise be bottlenecks. A West Coast insurance firm, for example, began using an evening part-time minishift in its claims examining, claims processing, and keypunching departments because they had no room to add daytime employees, and because the work output from these departments was necessary to the functioning of other departments the next day.

Job sharing is a part-time employment model in which two people share one full-time job. (Usually each works half-time, but other divisions are possible.) For example: (1) one person may work mornings and the other afternoons or (2) one may work Monday through Wednesday

Exhibit 2. Permanent part-time employment models in use, 1977.

Permanent Part-Time Employment Model	Percent of All Users (n=391)
Part days – five days a week or fewer	75
Full days – part week or part month	49
Minishift – short shift after full-time shift	23
Job sharing – full-time job divided between two part-time employees	22
Part-time employees do jobs that	
— require less than full time to complete	68
— are too much for full-time workers	29

Notes: Percent total exceeds 100 because model categories are not mutually exclusive (for example, minishift workers are also part-day workers), and because an organization with many part-time employees may use more than one model. The sample size is less than the total number of respondents in this and other exhibits because not all respondents answered all questions.

and the other may work Thursday and Friday or (3) one may work one week and one the next. Of course, job sharing requires that the two people work well together and coordinate their activities. This requirement naturally mandates a conscious match-up between the two workers and also between the job and the job-sharing model. For the employer, the unique potential benefit from job sharing lies in improved work performance arising from complementary aspects of the two job holders (one worker's weaknesses can be offset by the other worker's strengths, for example, or two heads are better than one), better coverage (when one worker is absent, the other can fill in or be available), and less disruption of work when one worker resigns (because the other remains to train a replacement). Examples of job sharing include a husband/wife team of librarians in an eastern county library and a pair of social case workers in a western city.

Neither job sharing nor part-time minishifts are commonly used. But they are used sufficiently often to be regarded as viable, serious part-time options. Among all responding organizations that used permanent part-time employment in 1977, about 22 percent used job sharing and 23 percent used part-time minishifts. The use of job sharing and minishifts appears about as frequently in one industry as another—given that some form of part-time employment is used—

except that job sharing may be slightly more common in wholesale and retail trades and minishifts slightly less common in government.

Part-time employment may be used when there is a nonstandard size of workload—work that is either less than or more than a full-time workload. (It is not always easy to distinguish the two, since work that is more than what one full-time person can do may also be thought of as less than two full-time jobs.) In the perception of respondents who use permanent part-time workers, more than two-thirds use them in jobs that require less than full-time to complete.

Usage Patterns for Permanent Part-Time Employment

The fact that there are proportionately more part-time employees in some industries (especially service industries and the wholesale and retail trades) and proportionately fewer in others (most notably manufacturing) is discussed in the Introduction and is documented by aggregate U.S. data (see U.S. Bureau of Labor Statistics, 1977). Additional usage patterns—depending on the size of female employment in the organization, the degree of labor union membership, and the organization's operating schedule and work technology—emerge from this survey.

Female Employment

Users of permanent part-time employment

Exhibit 3. Differences between 481 users and 228 non-users of permanent part-time employment, U.S., 1977.

Characteristic	Users (percent)	Non-Users (percent)
Female Employment		
less than 10 percent	3	11
10 to 24 percent	16	35
25 to 50 percent	40	37
more than 50 percent	41	17
Labor Union Membership		
none	56	41
1 to 24 percent	15	16
25 to 75 percent	25	32
more than 75 percent	4	11
Work Technology		
office work	92	83
factory work	61	89
services produced	45	31
goods produced	38	56
mass production; assembly line	20	30
discrete tasks; job autonomy	27	21
continuity; job performance requires knowledge of what happens throughout the work day	33	23
extended hours of operation (evenings, weekends)	45	37
cyclical demand for output (daily, weekly, or monthly peaks)	52	38
nonstandard size of workload (work tasks require <8 or >8 but <16 hours to complete)	36	25

are much more likely than non-users to have a high proportion of women in their workforce: In 41 percent of responding organizations, more than half of the workforce was female; among non-users, this figure drops to 17 percent (see Exhibit 3).

Labor Union Membership

Users of permanent part-time employment are somewhat less likely than non-users are to have substantial labor union representation. More than half the users had no labor union membership at all, and just 29 percent—compared with 43 percent of the nonusers—had as

much as a quarter of their workforce represented by unions (see Exhibit 3). Of course, the differences between users and non-users of part-time employment in both the level of female employment and labor union membership may be traceable to the relatively low level of permanent part-time employment in manufacturing firms, which constituted a large share of the sample.

Operating Schedule

Users of part-time employment do not differ from non-users in their office operating schedules. For both groups, over 90 percent have an eight-hour day or less and work five days per week. Similarly, their plant operating schedules are the same as those of non-users in terms of hours and shifts per day. About 70 percent operate plants more than eight hours a day and about 77 percent use more than one shift per day. But users with plant operations are more likely than non-users to work more than five days a week, by a margin of 42 percent to 25 percent. That is, users are more likely to have extended workweeks.

Work Technology

Work technology refers not only to the nature of the job and what is required to do it (for example, production processes, communication requirements, and co-worker relationships), but also to external demands made on the work unit (for example, scheduling requirements or relationships with customers). There are many different dimensions along which to describe work technology and many different aspects that could be measured. In this survey, respondents were queried only on technology aspects that were *expected* to have an effect on the use of permanent part-time employment. (Expectations were based on previous indications by business people.)

Overall, not many work technologies that characterize an organization succeed in distinguishing users from non-users of part-time employment. (The measures of work technology are gross measures, describing the entire organization. If technologies of particular jobs were measured, however, greater differences would be likely to show up. See Nollen, Eddy, and Martin, 1978.) There appear to be just three such technologies. Compared with non-users, for example, organizations that use part-time employment are less likely to be engaged in factory work and more likely to be services producers rather than goods producers. Users are also significantly more likely to have a cyclical demand for their output (daily, weekly, or monthly peaks); over half of them report this technology. This means that the use of part-time employment is favored by scheduling problems. Here's an example: Banks with heavy midday, Monday morning, or Friday afternoon traffic can use part-time tellers during these peak hours to better match the workforce to the regularly fluctuating size of the workload.

Similarly, part-time employment may be more frequently used in organizations that have extended hours of operation (as in retail stores with evening or weekend hours), and in cases where a nonstandard size of workload—less than eight hours, or more than eight but less than 16 hours a day required to do a job—characterizes many of the jobs in the organization. Differences here between users and non-users, however, are not large and not statistically significant.

Because part-time employment accounts for only a small proportion of total employment in the organizations that use it (see Exhibit 4), other work technologies that might be reported do not give much information. For example, previous studies have suggested that mass production/assembly line technologies and jobs with continuity demands are unfavorable to part-time employment because part-time workers are not present and on the job at all hours. On the other hand, jobs characterized by discrete tasks are considered especially well-suited to the nature of part-time work (see Nollen, Eddy, and Martin, 1978). In these survey results, however, no statistically significant differences between users and non-users of permanent part-time employment appeared for the above technologies—perhaps because they could be measured only as characteristics of most jobs in the organization rather than as they appeared in part-time versus full-time jobs.

Use with Other Alternative Work Schedules

Users of permanent part-time employment are more likely to use other alternative work schedules than are non-users. Both flexitime and compressed workweeks are found more often in organizations that use permanent part-time employment than in those that don't. Users of part-time employment are also somewhat more likely to have considered or to be planning the use of flexitime or compressed workweeks (see Exhibit 5). Thus alternative work schedules appear to complement each other rather than substitute for each other.

Exhibit 4. Proportion of permanent part-time employees in user organizations, by industry (percent distribution).

Industry	Percent of Employees on Permanent Part-Time			
	<1	1 to 4	5 to 25	>25
Manufacturing (n=180)	44	43	12	2
Transportation, communication, utilities (n=39)	31	51	—— 18 ——	
Wholesale and retail trade (n=29)	—— 28 ——		34	38
Finance, insurance, and real estate (n=95)	18	40	38	4
Service industries (n=49)	—— 35 ——		51	14
Government (n=25)	40	44	—— 16 ——	

Where Is Permanent Part-Time Employment Used in the Organization? Where Is It Not Feasible?

When part-time employment is used in an organization, its use is usually restricted to certain work units or job categories and to a small proportion of the total workforce. For example, part-time employment was used in most or all work units in only 17 percent of the user organizations. Less than 5 percent of the workforce were part-time employees among more than two-thirds of the users: Among 29 percent of the users, 1 percent or less of the workforce was part time. On the average, 6 to 9 percent of a user's workforce was part-time in this sample. More than three-quarters of the users of part-time employment have only non-exempt workers on a part-time basis. (Non-exempt employees are those covered by wage and hours legislation which, for example, requires the payment of overtime for time worked beyond eight hours a day or 40 hours a week. Exempt employees not covered by such legislation are usually those in professional or managerial jobs or in high level clerical or field sales jobs.)

The proportion of a user's workforce that is

Exhibit 5. Frequency of use of other alternative work schedules by part-time employment users and non-users.

Item	Part-Time Users (percent)	Part-Time Non-Users (percent)
Use of Part-Time Employment with Flexitime		
Use Flexitime	30	15
Have considered or are planning use of flexitime	26	17
Discontinued flexitime	2	2
Do not use flexitime	42	66
Use of Part-Time Employment with the Compressed Workweek		
Use compressed workweek	21	14
Have considered or are planning use of compressed workweek	22	8
Discontinued compressed workweek	9	8
Do not use compressed workweek	48	70

Note: Sample sizes are n=466 part-time users and n=224 part-time non-users. Usage percentages may be used for comparisons, but are not valid absolute estimates of usage. See the Introduction and Section 1 of this report and Section 1 and Appendix A of *Part 1: Flexitime,* Nollen and Martin, 1978.

working part time appears to vary dramatically according to the industry of the user. Isolated use occurs in manufacturing, transportation, communication, utilities, and government users—and most of these organizations that use permanent part-time employment have less than 5 percent of their workforce on a permanent part-time basis. However, more widespread use throughout user organizations is found in both wholesale and retail trade and in service industries. A sizable majority of users in these industries have more than 5 percent of their workforce on a permanent part-time basis (see Exhibit 4).

The most frequent use of permanent part-time employment in this sample (49 percent of all users) was among clerical or office workers (for example, secretary, file clerk, bookkeeper, bank teller, claims examiner, machine operator). Fewer users (10 to 20 percent) have part-time employment among professional employees (for example, lab technician, computer programmer, data-processing worker, translator, librarian, editorial staff, nursing staff, medical services staff), plant or production workers, retail sales clerks, or service workers or laborers (those, for example, in security, maintenance, customer service, or food service jobs). See Exhibit 6. (The relatively low number of part-time sales clerks and service workers in this sample results from the relatively large number of manufacturing firms in the sample.)

Exhibit 6. Where permanent part-time employment is and is not used.

Permanent Part-Time Employment Is Used:	Percent of 391 Users
in most or all units in the organization (whole company, division, or branch)	17
in clerical or office jobs	49
in professional jobs	17
in plant or production jobs	12
in sales or store clerk jobs	11
for service workers or laborers	9
for exempt employees only	3
for non-exempt employees only	76
for both exempt and non-exempt employees	21
by less than one percent of the workers	29
by 1 to 4 percent	39
by 5 to 9 percent	13
by 10 to 25 percent	13
by more than 25 percent	6

Permanent Part-Time Employment Is Not Feasible:	Percent of 178 Responses
for managers, supervisors, or professionals	34
where continuity is important; for example, continuous workflow, spontaneous communication needs	25
where there are high skill, high training, high product knowledge needs; technical jobs	16
for plant or production jobs	11
where public contact or customer service is required	5

Note: The average proportion of the workforce on permanent part-time employment in this sample is 6 to 9 percent.

Exhibit 7. Labor union membership among permanent part-time workers by industry (percent of users with low and high membership).

Industry	Proportion of Part-Time Workers Who Are Union Members	
	Low: none or less than 10 percent	High: more than 25 percent
Manufacturing (n=17)	94	3
Transportation, communication, and utilities (n=33)	79	21
Wholesale and retail trade (n=28)	64	29
Finance and insurance (n=76)	99	0
Services (n=37)	87	8
Government (n=22)	82	9

Where is permanent part-time employment not used? For what kinds of work activities is it not feasible? According to experienced users of part-time employment, there is no single one or two work activities for which part-time employment is ill suited. Nearly a third of the users mentioned none. Among the other users, four areas were mentioned occasionally. They are (1) managerial, supervisory, or professional jobs, cited as not feasible for part-time employment by 34 percent of the users; (2) jobs where continuity is important, mentioned by 25 percent; (3) jobs where there are high skill, high training, or high product-knowledge needs, suggested by 16 percent, and (4) plant or production jobs, mentioned by 11 percent of the users.

In managers' own words, part-time employment is not feasible:

- "Where functions are interrelated, whenever equipment must be operated continuously" (from a large eastern publishing house).
- "In management positions. We feel that full-time employees in management positions create greater continuity" (from a medium-size mid-Atlantic bank).
- "Generally for higher-skilled jobs requiring lengthy training" (from a large eastern bank).
- "For exempt level jobs where training and start-up costs are too high to warrant part-time investment. For factory jobs because of union contract" (from a small industrial manufacturer in the Midwest).

- "Probably not for first-line supervisors who follow daily workflow" (from a large western insurance company).
- "Shift operations—requirement of full complement of trained personnel. Crew work—need full time to make up crew" (from a large midwestern utility).
- "Creative-type functions—idea-producing jobs—where time to complete job is not predictable. . ." (from a small unit of municipal government in the East.

Obviously, then, non-use of part-time employment is associated with jobs considered ill suited to its use; not so obvious, however, is that non-use is also associated with labor union membership. Among nine out of ten users, less than 10 percent of the part-time employees were union members. By contrast, union membership was more common in the overall workforce of users—only six out of ten of the users had as little as 10 percent of their total workforce in labor unions. (see Exhibit 7.) On the average, about 6 percent of all part-time employees in this sample were union members while about 15 to 20 percent of all employees in user organizations were union members. Thus, unionized companies are both less likely to use permanent part-time employment at all and less likely to include union members as part-time workers even if they do use the system.

Part-time workers were more likely to be union members in some industries than in others. In both the finance/insurance and manufacturing industries, union membership among part-time workers was nil (either no union members or less than 10 percent with union membership) in almost all user organizations—99 and 94 percent respectively. However, in the wholesale/retail trade and transportation/communication/utilities industries, some users had substantial union membership among their part-time workers—29 and 21 percent of them, respectively, reported union membership among more than a quarter of their part-time workers.

3
Effects of Permanent Part-Time Employment on the Organization

Permanent part-time employment has several important effects on the organizations that use it—on job performance, on management practices, and on a variety of costs. What are these effects? Which are the good effects and which are the bad effects? Are these effects favorable overall?

Experiences of Users of Permanent Part-Time Employment

According to the experience of 460 user organizations, permanent part-time employment has good effects on several aspects of job performance, and it reduces labor costs. It also has mixed effects on management and occasionally increases some personnel costs. These conclusions and the findings below are based on opinion reports from users of part-time employment. The opinions are usually impressionistic; in only 20 to 30 percent of the cases are they based on actual collection of data—whether in-house surveys or analysis of personnel records. For the most part, then, they are based on managers' observations.

Effects on Job Performance

Part-time employment increases productivity and decreases worker fatigue among roughly 60 percent of the organizations that use it; almost no users report worse results. Absenteeism is

lower almost half the time, turnover is lower among 40 percent of the users (twice as often as it is higher), and tardiness is also lower because of part-time employment about two-fifths of the time (see Exhibit 8). Thus, according to each of a variety of measures of job performance, part-time employment is likely to be advantageous to organizations.

Effects on Communication

Because part-time workers are not on the job all day every day, concerns have been raised about communication problems. In fact, 35 percent of all the users of part-time employment in this survey reported that part-time employment worsened internal communication. Although this is not a large number, it constitutes one of the few overall negative effects of permanent part-time employment revealed in this survey. Communication outside the organization was not negatively affected, as Exhibit 8 shows.

Effects on Management Aspects

Part-time employment has diverse effects on management aspects; outcomes appear to be situation-specific. For example, coverage of work situations is made easier because of part-time employment in just over half the cases—perhaps because it solves problems of peak demand or extended hours of operation. Correspondingly, improvement in work scheduling is

Exhibit 8. Effects of permanent part-time employment on the organization: Experiences of 460 users, U.S., 1977.

Nature of Effects	Changes Attributed to Part-Time Employment (percent of all users)		
	Better	No Change	Worse
Effects on Job Performance			
Productivity	62	33	5
Turnover	40	41	19
Absenteeism	47	47	6
Tardiness	39	56	5
Fatigue	59	40	1
Effects on Communication			
Internal communication	6	59	35
External communication	6	76	18
Effects on Management Aspects			
Coverage of work situations	56	22	22
Employee scheduling	35	30	35
Work scheduling	41	29	30
Difficulty of management job	14	48	38
Effects on Costs			
Unit labor costs of production	52	42	6
Straight wage costs	58	39	3
Overtime costs	69	29	2
Fringe benefit costs	57	25	19
Personnel administration costs	16	45	39
Recruiting	46	37	17
Training	12	55	33
Equipment and facilities costs	15	71	14
Effects on Workers, Customers, Suppliers, and the Public			
Relationship with employees	31	56	13
Relationship with customers	12	78	10
Relationship with suppliers	3	89	8
Public relations	24	72	4

also frequently cited under part-time employment. Nevertheless, there are also quite a few reports of worsened coverage and work scheduling (22 and 30 percent of all users, respectively)—results that may stem from the regular absence of part-time workers from the job site during a part of the day or week. In addition, employee scheduling is worsened as often as it is improved (35 percent of all users in each case), and the overall difficulty of the management job is increased in 38 percent of the user organizations. As Exhibit 8 shows, however, no change was noted in nearly half the cases. Thus permanent part-time employment seems to require additional management effort in a substantial (but minority) number of cases; in turn, however, coverage of work situations and work scheduling are often improved. There are, however, often work situations (though these instances are less frequent) where such coverage is worsened, so no general conclusion can be drawn.

Effects on Costs

Part-time employment is responsible for reducing overtime costs and straight wage costs for a sizable majority of its users. Such savings are possible because the use of part-time employment enables an organization to have a closer match between the size of its workforce and the size of its workload. There may also be some degree of wage discrimination against part-time workers (see Owen, 1978 and Nollen, Eddy, and Martin, 1978)—more likely in the form of occupational discrimination (they get poorer jobs and no promotion) than in the form of unequal pay for equal work. In addition, the cost of fringe benefits for part-time workers is actually less than for full-time workers in a majority of cases—simply because not all fringe benefits are provided (see Exhibit 8). But in 19 percent of the cases, fringe benefit costs were *proportionately* higher (as they would be if all benefits were offered in full), and for 25 percent of the users they were the same for part-time workers as for full-time workers (the case when benefits are pro-rated to hours and/or earnings worked). Overall, as Exhibit 8 shows, unit labor costs of production were lower for part-time than for full-time employment for 52 of the organizations that used it, and higher for only 6 percent.*

Although part-time employment as currently used has a generally favorable effect on labor costs, it has a partially offsetting effect on personnel administration costs—39 percent of all users reported that these costs were higher because of part-time employment. One reason for this, possibly, is that special records may need to be kept for them. Training costs were increased for part-time employment among a third of all users, but were unaffected for more than half of them (since training for part-time workers beyond job familiarization is not often undertaken). Recruiting costs were often lower for part-time than for full-time workers, perhaps because of their excess supply as well as their reduced turnover.

Other Effects

Neither relationships with customers and suppliers nor relationships with the public were affected by part-time employment. Relationships among employees themselves were improved about a third of the time.

Analysis of Experiences with Permanent Part-Time Employment: Industry, Occupation, Part-Time Model, and Other Variables

Part-time employment is used more frequently in some industries and for some occupations than others. Are employers' experiences better in those industries and for those occupations? Several different part-time employment models are in use—including part-day, part-week, the minishift, and job sharing. Do some models give better results than others?

Below, the overall effects of part-time employment on the organization are analyzed. Key experiences are reported for individual industries, work units or occupational groups, and part-time employment models. By comparing these experiences across groups, we can suggest where part-time employment is most likely to be successful and why certain effects turn out to be good while others do not. The key effects to be analyzed are (1) productivity (a leading job-performance indicator and benefit of part-time employment); (2) management aspects—including coverage of work situations and work scheduling (both often improved but sometimes made worse), difficulty of the management job (often made worse), and internal communication (also often made worse); and (3) wage costs, fringe benefit costs, overtime costs, and unit labor costs of production (all favorable under part-time employment). (See Exhibit 9.)

Industry and Work Technology

Experiences with part-time employment may vary somewhat by industry, but the differences are small (see Exhibit 10). Firms in the industry with the least use of part-time employment—manufacturing—report less favorable results from

*Note in Exhibit 8 that the number of users reporting reduced unit labor costs was somewhat smaller than that of those reporting either increased productivity or reduced overtime, wage, or fringe benefit costs. Since only 16 percent of the users had collected data on unit labor costs, but a fourth had collected data on productivity and a third had collected data on labor compensation, the effect of part-time employment on reducing unit labor costs may be subjectively underestimated.

Exhibit 9. The good and bad effects of permanent part-time employment[a]: Experiences of 460 users, U.S., 1977.

Good Effects[b]	Bad Effects[c]	Effects Often Good, Sometimes Bad[d]
Reduces overtime	Worsens internal communication	Coverage of work situations
Increases productivity	Makes management job more difficult	Fringe benefits
Reduces fatigue		Work scheduling
Reduces straight wage costs	Increases personnel administration costs	Employee scheduling
Reduces unit labor costs		
Reduces absenteeism	Increases training costs	

Notes:

[a]In approximate order from strongest to weakest.

[b]Half or more of all users attributed better results to part-time employment, with few or no worse results reported.

[c]One-third or more users attributed worse results to part-time employment, with few better results reported.

[d]One-third to half or more of all users attributed better results to part-time employment, but a fifth to a third also reported worse results.

part-time employment when it is used than do users in the high-use industries of wholesale and retail trade, and finance and insurance. Manufacturing users, for example, less frequently experience improved productivity and coverage, and less frequently report lower labor compensation and unit labor costs stemming from part-time employment than do other users. On the other hand, firms in wholesale and retail trade and in finance and insurance usually report better-than-average results. Users in the service industries (other high-use industries) most not-

Exhibit 10. Industry differences in experiences with permanent part-time employment.

Experiences	Industry			
	Manu-facturing	Wholesale/Retail Trade	Finance, Insurance	Services
Experiences That Are Often Good	Percent Reporting Better Experiences			
Productivity	58	67	68	53
Coverage of work situations	50	79	62	53
Work scheduling	35	40	46	47
Unit labor costs	46	61	63	44
Straight wage costs	57	72	62	58
Overtime costs	67	80	77	73
Fringe benefit costs	61	66	62	50
Experiences That Are Sometimes Bad	Percent Reporting Worse Experiences			
Difficulty of management job	35	39	47	38
Internal communications	36	29	31	48

Notes: Sample sizes are n=175 for manufacturing, n=30 for wholesale and retail trade, n=107 for finance and insurance, and n=58 for services. Differences among industries are not statistically significant.

ably report improved work scheduling because of more frequent problems with uneven demand for output in the service industries. Other experiences for service industries are erratic, perhaps because of the heterogeneous nature of this large industry grouping.

A better understanding of permanent part-time employment experiences might be obtained by relating those experiences to work technology—to the nature of the job and production process and to the nature of external demands placed on the work unit. However, because part-time employees typically constitute a small proportion of a user's workforce while the descriptions of the user's work technology in this survey apply to the organization more globally, only a few valid inferences can be drawn.

First, users whose operations are characterized by the two work technologies that often explain why part-time employment is used—peaks in demand for output and extended hours of operation—may achieve better coverage of work situations and easier work scheduling somewhat more often than other users (see Exhibit 11). Second, users among service producers (regardless of their industry) report that permanent part-time employment improves work scheduling more often than goods producers do. These results suggest that part-time employment does indeed help managers cope with problems of uneven work flows. Third, part-time employment may increase productivity more often in work units that produce services rather than goods, that have unit production rather than mass

production processes, and that are characterized by a high level of strain (see Exhibit 12). These differences, although theoretically expected, are empirically small. A detailed analysis using better data would be required to establish such relationships.

Occupation

The frequency of reporting both key good experiences and key bad experiences with part-time employment varies substantially, depending on the occupation of the part-time workers. Overall, clerical part-time workers are more likely to give good results than are either professional or production part-time workers. However, part-time production workers were their equal in several respects. For example, 71 percent of all users of both part-time clerical and part-time production workers experienced improved productivity. Part-time clerical employment also excelled in reducing labor costs, including straight wage costs and overtime costs. On the other hand, part-time professional employment usually did not result in either reduced straight wage costs or unit labor costs (see Exhibit 13).

Part-Time Employment Models

A comparison of the key experiences with part-time employment for each of its different models separately revealed no significant differences. Whether in job performance, management aspects, or costs, none of the models examined—part-day, part-week, or minishift—

Exhibit 11. Effects of some work technologies on work coverage and scheduling experiences with permanent part-time employment.

Work Technology	Experience with Part-Time Employment (percent reporting better)	
	Coverage	Work Scheduling
Daily or weekly peaks in demand (n=242)	61	43
No daily or weekly peaks (n=139)	50	39
Extended hours of operation (n=205)	65	45
No extended hours (n=176)	48	37
Services producer (n=208)	60	49
Goods producer (n=176)	53	36

Exhibit 12. Effects of work technologies on productivity of permanent part-time workers.

Work Technology	Percent of Users Reporting Better Productivity
Services producer (n=206)	66
Goods producer (n=178)	57
Unit production process (n=71)	66
Mass production process (n=95)	58
Heavy mental or physical strain (n=110)	74
No heavy strain (n=271)	58

revealed any superiority. Since job sharing part-time workers are likely to be only a small fraction of all part-time workers in a user organization, no valid results for job sharing separately could be obtained in this study.

Expectations of Non-Users

Naturally enough, the experiences of organizations using part-time employment are, on balance, favorable—otherwise the organizations would not persist in its use. But what about employers who do not use part-time employment? Do they have generally unfavorable expectations of its effects? Do they see some potentially good experiences? (See Exhibit 14).

There are substantial differences between the *expectations of non-users* and the *experiences of users* concerning the effects of part-time employment on the organization. Most notably, non-users are pessimistic about the management aspects of part-time employment considerably more often than are users—and they believe such aspects are made worse in part-time situations compared with full-time employment in a majority of cases. Non-users are also less likely than users to perceive labor cost savings—their opinions are divided, whereas users were positive in more than half the cases. While there were also fewer non-users than users who expected good job performance results from part-time employment, they remained positive on balance.

Overall, non-users of permanent part-time employment identify the same bad effects that users report, but include others as well. Correspondingly, non-users identify fewer good effects but do include two of those reported by users. The leading bad effects that non-users of part-time employment expect from its use are that the management job will be made more difficult

Exhibit 13. Occupational differences in experiences with permanent part-time employment.

Experience	Occupation		
	Professional	Clerical	Production
Experiences That Are Often Good	Percent Reporting Better		
Productivity	53	71	71
Coverage	58	60	59
Work scheduling	38	46	33
Recruiting	37	46	52
Unit labor costs	28	60	50
Straight wage costs	37	66	45
Overtime costs	63	75	61
Fringe benefit costs	46	65	65
Experiences That Are Sometimes Bad	Percent Reporting Worse		
Difficulty of management job	29	35	32
Internal communications	41	29	29

Notes: Sample sizes are n=41 for professionals, n=145 for clerical, and n=31 for production workers. Other occupations such as sales workers or service workers either were too imprecisely defined or had too small a sample to be reported. Most differences among occupations are not statistically significant.

Exhibit 14. Expectations of 324 non-users on the effects of permanent part-time employment.

Nature of Effects	Expected Changes Attributed to Part-Time Employment (percent of all non-users)		
	Better	No Change	Worse
Effects on Job Performance			
Productivity	43	32	25
Turnover	35	34	32
Absenteeism	40	40	20
Tardiness	34	54	13
Fatigue	62	35	3
Effects on Communication			
Internal communication	3	38	59
External communication	3	58	40
Effects on Management Aspects			
Coverage of work situations	33	16	51
Employee scheduling	16	21	63
Work scheduling	19	20	61
Difficulty of management job	7	21	72
Effects on Costs			
Unit labor costs of production	34	35	31
Straight wage costs	41	51	8
Overtime costs	55	33	12
Fringe benefit costs	42	17	41
Personnel administration costs	7	25	68
Recruiting	37	30	32
Training	4	31	65
Equipment and facilities costs	8	66	26
Other Effects			
Relationship with employees	27	41	32
Relationship with customers	6	68	26
Relationship with suppliers	5	71	24
Public relations	23	68	9

and that personnel administration costs will be higher. These effects were also sometimes reported by users. But, in addition, a majority of non-users believe that training costs will be higher, which is less frequently reported by users, and that employee and work scheduling will be more difficult. In the experience of users, employee and work scheduling were more often made easier than more difficult.

As Exhibit 14 shows, the two good effects expected by non-users are less fatigue and reduced overtime payments. In addition, a substantial number of non-users expect reduced straight wage costs. But they are divided in their opinions about fringe benefit costs and unit labor costs of production—in contrast to the users, who found them to be reduced in a majority of cases.

Of course, differences between the experiences of users and the expectations of non-users of part-time employment might arise from differences in their industry and work technology—or simply from misperception. The answer seems to lie partly in both realms. Non-users, for example, were more likely to be either manufacturers or in finance and insurance than users were. They were less likely, however, to have uneven demand for output or extended hours of operation, or to be services producers as opposed to goods producers. Thus these organizations, if they were to use part-time employment, would experience good effects less frequently than the average for current users. However, the current users of permanent part-time employment who were in exactly these same industry or work technology situations reported good experiences more often than the non-users expected (compare Exhibits 14 and 10). Other effects that non-users expected to be unfavorable did not vary by industry or technology.

Thus it appears that some organizations not now using permanent part-time employment could do so and obtain generally favorable results, much as present users do. First, however, it is necessary to spread the word on what work situations are potentially profitable for the use of part-time employment.

4
Managing Permanent Part-Time Employment

Permanent part-time employment is used in many different ways and places. Experiences with it vary. Sometimes the manager's job is made harder because of part-time employment; other times it is made easier. Similarly, coverage and scheduling are made better in some organizations and worse in others. There is always a challenge to management in the successful use of permanent part-time employment.

In this chapter, attention is focused on the management of permanent part-time employment: where it originates, why it is adopted, how it is implemented and changed over time, how the key issues of fringe benefits and labor unions are handled, and what problems are encountered and how they are solved.

Why Permanent Part-Time Employment Is Implemented

The suggestion to use permanent part-time employment usually originates in personnel or personnel-related departments (46 percent of all users) or with top management itself (34 percent of all users). (It should be noted that the respondents themselves were personnel executives or other top managers.) Established employees and unions are only occasional sources for the suggestion to use permanent part-time employment.

Why do managers adopt part-time employment? Various good effects of part-time employment have been noted—reduced overtime, increased productivity, less fatigue, reduced straight wage costs, reduced unit labor costs, and reduced absenteeism, to cite the leading good effects (see the preceding section). However, a reported good effect may or may not be important to the employer and hence may or may not be decisive in explaining its use. When employers were asked the open-ended question, "Why do you use part-time employment?" the answers indicated a dominant reason: to solve a scheduling problem. Nearly three-quarters of all users offered this reason, among others (see Exhibit 15).

Scheduling Problems Solved

Scheduling problems solved by part-time employment are of several different kinds. They are illustrated best in managers' own words:

- "Often in a given department we do not need an additional full-time person, but have more work than can be done by the present workforce. Overtime is too costly, and we seldom use it" (from a medium-size manufacturing company in the Midwest).
- "Cost-effective handling of peak-period work" (from a large eastern bank).
- "Policyholder contact at night" (from a medium-size western life insurance firm).
- "Helpful in filling in for weekend duty—replace people who are scheduled off—we use regular 4-day-a-week or 2-day-a-week

Exhibit 15. Reasons for using permanent part-time employment.

Reason	Percent of All Users
Work scheduling assisted—match peak workloads or fit customer flow, extended hours of operation, job requires less than or more than full-time, give flexibility, cover specialized jobs	72
Labor supply and recruiting—utilize talent otherwise not available, use experienced employees, retain good employees, unique skills available	26
Reduce labor costs, more cost-effective	12
Reduce fringe benefit costs	3
Increase production—for example, by adding minishift	3
Provide employee benefit	4

Note: Percent total exceeds 100 because of multiple responses. Sample size is 380.

employees" (from a large hospital in the East).

- "It accomodates a management need—that of paying only for the time required to perform job functions, not for being present" (from a medium-size mid-Atlantic social action group).
- "Ability to achieve greater efficiency by scheduling employees to work during periods when needed" (from a large midwestern bank).
- "To accomplish ongoing tasks that require experience and job knowledge but do not justify a full-time position (from a small college in the East).

Other Advantages: Labor Supply and Worker Quality

The next most frequent set of reasons, mentioned by one-quarter of the users, referred to advantages associated with labor supply and worker quality. Here are some of the advantages cited:

- "Able to get better qualified workers and better employee morale" (from a small manufacturing company in the Midwest).
- "For our organization the main advantage has been continued partial employment of retired employees" (from a small midwestern manufacturing company).
- "Students in this category became permanent employees—good means of recruiting

full-time employees" (from a moderately small eastern manufacturing company).

- "Enriches staff by virtue of numbers" (from a small unit in a large midwestern university).
- "Complementary skills (one person doesn't have to have all the qualifications); support for each other" (from a small unit in a large university in the Pacific Northwest).
- "Allows the company to take advantage of a mature, stable market for new employees" (from a moderately large mid-Atlantic life insurance company).

Despite being good effects, productivity and labor cost improvements were infrequently mentioned as reasons for using part-time employment. Furthermore, as Exhibit 15 shows, fringe benefit savings were seldom mentioned. These results indicate that managers are not thinking strictly in terms of economic benefit/cost when they decide to use part-time employment. Rather, they appear to regard part-time employment as a solution to particular management problems—how to cope with awkward work demands, for example—and implement it on that basis. Subsequently favorable economic results enhanced it as a solution.

Implementation Steps

The list of implementation steps that can be taken once the idea is raised is long and varied—ranging from discussing permanent part-time plans with other organizations to documenting the quantitative results of a pilot program. The implementation steps can be broken down into a planning phase and an adoption phase. The planning phase includes all fact-finding and opinion-gathering steps and identification of internal management responsibilities. The adoption phase includes (1) changes instituted in organizational operations because of part-time employment as well as (2) the actual start-up of permanent part-time employment and (3) the possible measurement of its results.

The most important implementation news from this sample of permanent part-time users is that not many implementation steps are formally undertaken. In many cases, part-time employment appears to just "happen" instead of being consciously planned and implemented. For example, even the most commonly used implementation step in the planning phase (holding meetings with managers or supervisors) and in the adoption phase (instituting first on a trial basis) were taken by less than half the users of part-time employment—42 and 41 percent, respectively (see Exhibit 16).

Planning for part-time employment was seldom discussed with other organizations or with employees. Union representatives were consulted in half the cases where union members were among the part-time employees (17 users held meetings with union representatives, while 34 users had more than 10 percent union membership among their part-time employees). Neither outside seminars or conferences nor outside consultants were used, nor was an internal project director appointed except in rare instances. Just over a quarter of all users reviewed state and federal labor laws—including statutes on fringe benefits and payroll taxes applicable to part-time employment.

In the adoption phase, aside from the initial trial use of part-time employment, the most remarkable finding is the lack of results measurement. Only 9 percent of all users established baseline data for a formal evaluation of business results, and only 6 percent actually provided for an audit of the results after adoption. Just over a quarter of all users restructured work in some way to accomodate part-time employment.

Exhibit 16. Implementation steps taken by users of permanent part-time employment.

Implementation Steps	Percent of All Users
Planning Phase	
Held meetings with managers, supervisors	42
Reviewed state and federal labor laws	28
Discussed plan with other organizations	18
Held meetings with employees	12
Held meetings with union representatives	4
Appointed an internal project director	3
An organization member attended a seminar or conference	1
Engaged a consultant	<1
Adoption Phase	
Instituted first on a trial basis	41
Work restructured	27
Established baseline data for formal evaluation of	
—business results	9
—part-time employee attitudes	4
—full-time employee attitudes	2
Employees cross-trained	9
Provided for audit of results	6
Employees voted on adoption	1

Notes: Sample size is 380. Totals exceed 100 percent because of multiple responses.

Quite clearly, permanent part-time employment is not regarded as a major element in a firm's employment policy. Its implementation is seldom systematically planned and its effects on the organization are seldom systematically assessed. Its use must be justified on grounds other than a quantitative cost-benefit outcome.

Do the two frequently taken implementation steps yield any improvement in the results of part-time employment? That is, are the organizations reporting these two implementation steps also more likely to report better job performance, fewer management problems, or lower costs? In the case of organizations that instituted part-time employment first on a trial basis, the answer is yes—maybe. In the case of organizations

Exhibit 17. Experiences with permanent part-time employment in organizations that did and did not institute it first on a trial basis.

Experiences That May Have Been Improved by Instituting Part-Time Employment First on a Trial Basis	Changes Attributed to Part-Time Employment (percent of all users)		
	Better	No Change	Worse
Productivity			
Instituted first on a trial basis	68	28	4
Did not institute first on a trial basis	59	36	5
Turnover			
Instituted first on a trial basis	51	31	18
Did not institute first on a trial basis	35	46	19
Absenteeism			
Instituted first on a trial basis	54	37	7
Did not institute first on a trial basis	45	49	6
Tardiness			
Instituted first on a trial basis	45	50	5
Did not institute first on a trial basis	36	59	5
Difficulty of the Management Job			
Instituted first on a trial basis	20	49	31
Did not institute first on a trial basis	12	47	41
Coverage			
Instituted first on a trial basis	63	18	19
Did not institute first on a trial basis	52	25	23
Work Scheduling			
Instituted first on a trial basis	44	26	30
Did not institute first on a trial basis	39	28	33
Straight Wage Costs			
Instituted first on a trial basis	64	33	3
Did not institute first on a trial basis	49	47	4
Overtime Costs			
Instituted first on a trial basis	78	21	1
Did not institute first on a trial basis	65	33	2
Fringe Benefit Costs			
Instituted first on a trial basis	66	17	17
Did not institute first on a trial basis	52	28	20

Notes: The sample size for the two groups is 145 and 225, respectively. Differences between the two groups are not statistically significant.

that held meetings with managers and supervisors before adoption, there was no evidence of superior results in this study. Of course, these findings are quite rough since no other features of the users that might also affect their experiences could be simultaneously taken into account.

In comparison with full-time employment, implementation of permanent part-time employment by instituting it first on a trial basis was perhaps associated with modest increases in productivity and modest decreases in turnover, absenteeism, and tardiness. The trial basis was also associated with more favorable experiences with coverage, work scheduling, and the overall difficulty of the management job. And organizations proceeding first on a trial basis also reported lower wage costs, overtime costs, and fringe benefit costs more frequently than did other user organizations (see Exhibit 17). In all cases, however, the differences associated with this implementation step are quite small and statistically not very significant.

Once permanent part-time employment was implemented in the organization, few changes were made in the way in which it was used. Only 19 percent of all users reported any changes since part-time employment was begun. (Most users are long-term users—84 percent had used part-time employment more than three years, and 96 percent had used it more than one year.)

The only managerial modification of part-time employment reported several times was in the handling of fringe benefits. Some managers moved to include part-time employees in more fringe benefit offerings, while a few reduced the work hours of part-time employees to fewer than 20 per week in order to avoid their inclusion in pension plans as newly mandated by ERISA (see below).

The Role of Labor Unions

For the most part, labor unions are not involved in the implementation of part-time employment. Only about 6 percent of all part-time employees are union members and only one out of every ten organizations that use part-time employment have measurable union membership among their part-time workers. This low union involvement may be accounted for in part by the concentration of part-time workers in occupations that traditionally have had little union representation. It may also have resulted in part from actual or perceived opposition to part-time employment by unions.

Users' responses to open-ended questions about the role of labor unions in the adoption of part-time employment (such responses were offered by 10 percent of all users) were negative two times out of three. In some cases, collective bargaining agreements effectively bar part-time employment, and in other cases managers report that unions seek to limit part-time employment, in terms of total numbers or in specific jobs or situations. But there were also instances of initiating and participatory union roles, and other instances of at least passive acceptance. In a few cases, unions asked for part-time employment in the course of bargaining, and in other cases, the terms and condtions of part-time employment were made part of the union contract. (See Exhibit 18.)

Problems and Solutions

Among users of part-time employment who identified a problem with its use (37 percent of all users), two areas of difficulty occurred about a quarter of the time. They were problems with work or worker scheduling and problems with fringe benefits. (See Exhibit 19.) Scheduling problems included coverage, lack of continuity, difficult communication, complicated supervision, and problems of meshing the part-time worker's personal schedule with the workplace schedule. Fringe benefit problems included complaints from part-timers over more benefits, questions of how to offer equitable benefits, and the burden of compliance with state and federal regulations, especially with regard to ERISA provisions.

In addition, roughly 15 percent of the problems managers reported dealt with relationships between part-time and full-time employees—matters of equity in wage rates, seniority accumulation, layoff policy, and the use of space and equipment. A smaller number of managers encountered problems with turnover among part-time workers, recruiting them, or training

Exhibit 18. Labor union role in adoption of permanent part-time employment.

Role	Percent of Users
No role (includes users with no union and no part-time employees in union-represented area)	90
Positive or passive role	3
Negative role	7

Examples of positive roles:

"It helped them (unions) too, and they agreed to such employment in the collective bargaining agreement."

"Bargained for (permanent part-time employment) during process of negotiations."

"Wages, working conditions bargained with unions and stated in labor agreements."

"Helped establish ground rules."

"The manner in which part-time employees are utilized has become structured and changed through negotiations with the union."

"Agreed to this necessary alternative to full-time."

Examples of negative roles:

"Attempted to limit part-time." "They are trying to limit it."

"They are against it and continuously demanding curtailment."

"Union objected to (part-time employment). Renegotiated agreement and established percentage limits on (its) use."

"Won't allow within bargaining unit."

"Union contract won't allow."

"In all cases unions have opposed permanent part-time employees."

"They generally oppose their use, except where job need is very clearly less than full-time."

"(Part-time employment) could be feasible with our operation. However, the union tends to look on (it) with suspicion and as a means of lowering rates."

Notes: The sample size is 380 users of part-time employment.

them. Occasional difficulties were reported in securing cooperation and support from managers and supervisors, labor union opposition, recordkeeping burdens, and moonlighting among part-time workers.

Solutions to these problems were as varied as the problems themselves and do not fall into any general patterns. Examples of the problems encountered and their solutions, in the respondents' own words, are reported in Exhibit 20.

Why Do Some Organizations Decide Against Part-Time Employment?

The number of organizations in this survey that had discontinued part-time employment after a period of use was very small—only 1 percent of all one-time users. However, some knowledge of what blocks further use of part-time employment can be gained from the reasons non-users offered for deciding against its use and from the disadvantages they cite. From this small amount of evidence (about 95 open-ended responses), it appears that concerns about fringe benefits and about the commitment and loyalty of part-time workers are foremost. Anticipated scheduling problems and higher overhead costs (recruiting training, recordkeeping) are also frequently expressed.

The fringe benefit problem on the minds of most non-users is ERISA—as a large western

Exhibit 19. Problems encountered in the use of permanent part-time employment.

Problem	Percent of Responses
Work or worker scheduling—coverage, lack of continuity, communication, worker's availability, supervision	26
Fringe benefits—part-timers' desire for more benefits, how to offer equitable benefits, compliance with state, federal regulations	23
Part-time/full-time relationships—equity in wages, seniority, layoffs; use of equipment	15
Labor supply—recruiting, turnover, and training	10
Securing cooperation of managers, supervisors	5
Labor unions	5
Recordkeeping	5
Moonlighting	3
Other	8

Note: The sample size is responses from 141 users who described a problem and its solution in an open-ended question.

distribution company put it very simply, "ERISA requirements would increase benefits cost." Higher costs resulting from such other benefits as equitable health insurance are less worrisome. Some managers see an acceptable trade-off between the higher cost of benefits and higher productivity. The commitment problem that troubles non-users was summed up by a large eastern industrial manufacturing company as "The lack of a feeling of employee responsibility and accountability. Perhaps no real feeling that an employee 'belongs'." Other non-users were wary of "lack of total dedication to the job" (a large scientific services company). Since *users* of part-time employment seldom found lack of commitment, dedication, or loyalty to be a negative effect, there is an education task ahead if more organizations are to offer part-time jobs. There remains the view in many quarters, however, that "part-timers by nature are not permanent" (small unit of a large consumer manufacturing company located on the Pacific Coast).

Fringe Benefits

One aspect of part-time employment that requires management attention is that of fringe benefits. Many organizations do not pay all fringe benefits to part-time workers, but pressures are mounting to change these policies.

What fringe benefits are paid to permanent part-time workers? Vacation leave is by far the fringe benefit most frequently offered to permanent part-time employees—80 percent of all organizations made it available to their part-time employees in 1977, almost always on a prorated basis (half-time employees, for example, got half the vacation days per year that full-time employees received). Sick leave for part-time employees is also usually prorated to time worked, but in total only 55 percent of all organizations made it available to their part-time workers. (Since a few organizations did not allow sick leave for full-time employees either, the percentage of organizations discriminating against part-time workers with respect to sick leave was only 40 percent. (See Exhibit 21.) In some instances benefits may be limited to employees who work at least half time.

Life and health insurance plans were offered to permanent part-time workers by just over half the organizations employing them (almost all full-time employees received these benefits). The life insurance benefit was prorated in some

Exhibit 20. Examples of permanent part-time employment problems and their solutions (actual reports from users).

Problem	Solution
Work or worker scheduling problems	
Scheduling.	Realigned job duties.
Workflow.	Put part-time employees only in jobs where workflow is flexible.
Supervision on shifts after regular day work.	Special training sessions.
Loss of continuity with a 2- or 3-day week.	Part-timers work one week on, one week off. Other part-timers work alternate week.
Internal communication.	More formal time designated for debriefing and information-giving.
Staff communication.	All staff members are present one full day (the same day) weekly.
Performance evaluation.	Really haven't done a good job of solving it yet.
Career pathing.	We haven't solved it.
Fringe benefit problems	
Employees complained about no vacation or holiday pay.	Prorated schedule was implemented.
Dissatisfaction with no holiday pay in union contract.	Established eligibility every six-month period and prorated holiday to average hours worked in that time.
Desire for health insurance coverage.	Set minimum number of hours to be worked to qualify for coverage.
Proration of benefits because of varying number of hours worked per week.	We struck an average number of hours per week and prorated on this figure.
Benefits question re ERISA.	Holding to less than 1,000 hours/year.
ERISA.	Not solved yet, if ever.
Because of ERISA, we currently doubt this program can continue to utilize the same people.	Still not sure of outcome; however, will probably discontinue some activities.
Relationships between part-time and full-time employees	
Complaints re salary as compared with full-time.	Raise salary schedules to same as full-time ones.
Seniority status when layoffs occur. Do part-timers retain seniority over full-time?	Negotiate solution on an individual basis.
Grievances on seniority accrued and eligibility for regular full-time job.	Resolved through grievance procedure.
Conflicts developed between full-time and part-time employees working on the same machines.	This is not completely solved.

29

Exhibit 20 (continued).

Problem	*Solution*
Problems with cooperation and support from managers or supervisors	
Gaining managerial acceptance; convincing management to try it.	Initiated trial program and allowed manager to be deeply involved in evaluation of both productivity and impact on other employees.
Widespread attitudinal resistance at management, supervisory levels.	Developing video training module to to condition new attitudes.
Supervisors accepting part time in lieu of full-time employee.	Convinced them to try it; they found they could get by with a part-time instead of a full-time person.
Many managers not willing to make extra effort to restructure work for part-timers.	We have tried to point out that cost savings and productivity make this worthwhile.
Supervisors had difficulty planning their work at first.	They soon learned to get clerical work done when stenographers were there and leave nonclerical needs (phone calls, research, visits) to hours when clerk not there.
Temporary help gets confused with permanent part-time help in the minds of supervisors.	Needed to get a good definition.
Problems with turnover and training	
High turnover.	Better salary administration program and expanded fringe benefits.
Turnover in part-time staff (mostly college students).	Not solved. We are considering trying to tap the retired worker.
Turnover and training costs high.	Learned to screen applicants for need to work this type of schedule.
Low attendance of part-time em-employees at inservice programs.	Attendance improved by paying them their hourly rate for attending on off-duty time (hospital).
Training.	Bring part-time employees on full-time for two weeks for on-the-job training.

fashion about half the time, while health insurance was prorated one-third of the time. In the remainder of cases, life and health insurance benefits were the same for part-time as for full-time workers. Pension benefits were offered to part-time employees by 59 percent of their employers (prorated in more than two-thirds of the cases); they were offered to full-time employees by 93 percent of these same organizations.

Some form of profit sharing was offered to part-time employees by only 28 percent of the user organizations. This figure contrasts with a majority of organizations—61 percent—offering this benefit to full-time workers.

ERISA. Among all fringe benefits, the one that stirs the most comment from employers and is potentially the most difficult to reconcile with part-time employment is retirement plans. The reason for this is ERISA—the Employee Retirement Income Security Act of 1974.*

*Material in this section is based on Nollen, Eddy, and Martin, 1978.

Exhibit 21. Fringe benefits paid to permanent part-time employees.

Fringe Benefit	Offered to Full-Timers	Offered to Part-Timers		
		Total	Prorated	Same as Full-Time
		(percent of all users of part-time employment)		
Vacation	99	80	75	5
Sick Leave	95	55	49	6
Life Insurance	96	51	27	24
Health Insurance	97	52	19	33
Pension	93	59	42	17
Profit Sharing	61	28	20	8

Note: The sample size was 387 users of permanent part-time employment.

In general, an employer's contribution to the pension plan for an employee is based on that person's earnings, and is therefore proportionally the same for full-time and part-time employees. But the dollar cost of the considerable individual recordkeeping that retirement plans necessitate is the same for full-time as for part-time workers —so administrative cost is proportionally higher for part-time employees.

The advent of ERISA has not caused employers who already include permanent part-time employees in their retirement plans to make any special adjustments. But it has been of concern to some employers who exclude part-time workers. ERISA guards against pension plan abuse and provides pension portability to workers who change employers. If pension plans are to qualify for tax-exempt status, it requires them to meet minimum standards for participation (employee eligibility), funding (employer contribution), and vesting (transfer of ownership of accrued contributions from the plan to the employees).

The general rule of particular concern to those who employ workers is the stipulation that otherwise qualified employees who work 1,000 or more hours a year (about half time or more) must all be treated alike—that is, included in an organization's pension plan (if it has one), made eligible to receive employer contributions based on annual earnings, and eventually made eligible for full vesting (100 percent ownership of employer contributions as well as any employee contributions). Contributions for part-time

employees are modest since they are based on annual earnings and, in some cases, are paid only on compensation above a certain amount. Once placed in the pension fund, however, they are not recoverable and pass entirely from the employer's control.

Since many employers view pensions as retirement income provided to long-term and faithful employees, they are often unwilling to assume either the administrative or the financial responsibility that including large numbers of part-time employees would entail. Of course, this argument implies that part-time employees are also regarded as short-term employees.

Some employers exclude part-time workers simply by limiting the number of hours these employees may work to fewer than 1,000 per year. However, the law itself recognizes the legitimacy of concentrating retirement benefits on long-term employees and allows employers considerable latitude in setting participation standards, contribution formulae, and vesting schedules that exclude short-term, full-time *and* part-time employees. For example, the retirement plan may include only salaried personnel. Participation may be limited to those who meet a one-year minimum service requirement and may be postponed until an employee is 25 years old.

ERISA also allows employers to establish a minimum compensation requirement. Employer contributions then need not be made for participating employees unless their annual compensation exceeds a specified amount.

Bibliography

1. Association of American Colleges, Project on the Status and Education of Women, *Part Time Faculty Employment* (Washington, D.C.: 1976).

2. Bednarzik, Robert W., "Part-Time Work and Public Policy," unpublished Ph.D. dissertation, University of Missouri, forthcoming.

3. Bennet, B.A., "Part Time Nursing Employment in Great Britain," *International Labor Review,* April 1962.

4. Bruntz, T., "Part-Time Employment of Women in Industrial Countries," *International Labor Review,* November 1962.

5. Bureau of National Affairs, *Bulletin to Management: ASPA-BNA Survey No. 25—Part-Time and Temporary Employees* (Washington, D.C.: Bureau of National Affairs, December 5, 1974).

6. Catalyst, Inc., *Part-Time Teachers and How They Work: A Study of Five School Systems* (New York: 1968).

7. California Senate. Select Committee on Investment Priorities and Objectives, Hearings, "Leisure-sharing," November 1, 1977.

8. Clark, Robert, *Adjusting Hours to Increase Jobs* (Washington, D.C.: National Commission for Manpower Policy, 1977).

9. College and University Personnel Association, "Alternative Work Schedules," *Journal of the College and University Personnel Association,* Summer 1977.

10. Control Data Corporation, "Part-Time Employment in Bindery Operations" (Minneapolis: 1973).

11. Darrow, Susan T., and Stokes, Sybil L., "Part-Time Professional and Administrative Employment at the University of Michigan" (Ann Arbor: University of Michigan, Center for Continuing Education of Women, January 1973).

12. Daski, Robert S., "Area Wage Survey Test Focuses on Part-Timers," *Monthly Labor Review,* April 1974.

13. Flynt, Jerry, "Growing Part-Time Work Force Has Major Impact on Economy," *New York Times,* April 12, 1977.

14. Greenwald, Carol, and Liss, J., "Part-Time Workers Can Bring Higher Productivity," *Harvard Business Review,* September 1973.

15. Gruber, Alan Robert, "A Comparative Study of the Utilization of Mature College Graduated Women Employed Half Time as Caseworkers in an Urban Public Welfare Department," Ph.D. dissertation, Columbia University, 1971.

16. Haldi Associates, Inc. *Alterative Work Schedules: A Technology Assessment,* RANN Grant No. 10-40456 (Washington, D.C.: National Science Foundation, ASRA Information Resources Center, 1977).

17. Hallaire, Jean, *Part-Time Employment: Its Extent and Its Problems* (Paris: Organization for Economic Cooperation and Development, 1968).

18. _____, "Working Hours per Week and Day," *New Patterns for Working Time,* Supplement to the Final Report (Paris: Organization for Economic Cooperation and Development, 1973).

19. Hewes, Amy, "Women Part-Time Workers in the United States," *International Labor Review,* November 1962.

20. Howell, Margaret A., and Ginsburg, Marjorie G., "Evaluation of the Professional and Executive Corps of the Department of Health, Education and Welfare," *Public Personnel Management,* January 1973.

21. International Labor Office, "An International Survey of Part-Time Employment," Parts I and II, *International Labor Review,* October and November 1963.

22. International Labor Office, *Part-Time Employment: An International Survey,* W.4 (Geneva: 1973).

23. International Labor Office, "Part-Time Employment for Women with Family Responsibilities," *International Labor Review,* June 1957.

24. Janjic, Marion, "Part-Time Work in Public Service," *International Labor Review,* April 1972.

25. Jones, Ethel B., "Women and Part-Week Work" (Springfield, Virginia: National Technical Information Service, forthcoming).

26. Klein, Viola, *Women Workers: Working Hours and Services: A Survey in Twenty-One Countries* (Paris: Organization for Economic Cooperation and Development, 1965).

27. Laser, Ellen A., *Constructing an Employee Benefit Package for Part-Time Workers* (New York: Catalyst, Inc., 1975).

28. Lazer, Robert I., "Job Sharing as a Pattern for Permanent Part-Time Work," *The Conference Board Record,* October 1975.

29. Levitan, Sar, and Belous, Richard, *Shorter Hours, Shorter Weeks: Spreading the Work to Reduce Unemployment* (Baltimore: John Hopkins University Press, 1977).

30. Lobes, Carol, Chief of Federal Manpower Programs Section, Wisconsin State Bureau of Human Resource Services, Testimony to the California Senate Select Committee on Investment Priorities and Objectives, November 1, 1977.

31. Lynton, Edith F., *Alternatives to Layoffs* (New York: New York City Commission on Human Rights, 1975).

32. Main, Jeremy, "Good Jobs Go Part-Time," *Money,* October 1977.

33. Martin, Virginia H., *Hours of Work When Workers Can Choose: The Experience of 59 Organizations with Employee-Chosen Staggered Hours and Flexitime* (Washington, D.C.: Business and Professional Women's Foundation, 1975).

34. McCarthy, Maureen E., *The Extent of Alternative Work Schedules in State Government* (Washington, D.C.: Committee for Alternative Work Patterns, 1977).

35. Morse, Dean, *The Peripheral Worker* (New York: Columbia University Press, 1969).

36. National Center for Productivity and Quality of Working Life, *Alternatives in the World of Work* (Washington, D.C.: 1976).

37. Nollen, Stanley D.; Eddy, Brenda B.; and Martin, Virginia H., *Permanent Part-Time Employment: An Interpretive Review* (Springfield, Virginia: National Technical Information Service, 1977).

38. _____, *Part-Time Employment: The Manager's Perspective* (New York: Praeger Publishers, Inc., 1978).

39. Novitski, A., and Babkina, M., "Part Time Work and Employment," *Problems of Economics,* January 1974.

40. Owen, John D., "An Econometric Analysis of the Part-Time Labor Market in the United States" (Springfield, Virginia: National Technical Information Service, 1978).

41. Prywes, Ruth W., *Study on the Development of a Non-Standard Workday or Workweek for Women* (Springfield, Virginia: National Technical Information Service, 1974).

42. Sandberg, Mark E., "A Study of Attitudes, Values and Expressed Satisfaction of Part-Time Employers in Hospitals," unpublished Ph.D. dissertation, Cornell University, 1971.

43. Sandler, Rhoda and Platt, Judith, "Job Sharing at Montgomery County," *Library Journal,* November 1973.

44. Sawyer, Kathy, "Time Out: America Begins to Work Less," *Washington Post,* December 25, 26, 27, and 28, 1977.

45. Schonberger, Richard J., "Ten Million U.S. Housewives Want to Work," *Labor Law Journal,* June 21, 1970.

46. Schwartz, Jane, *Part-Time Employment: Employer Attitudes on Opportunities for the College Trained Woman* (New York: Alumnae Advisory Center, Inc., 1964).

47. Seear, B., *Reentry of Women to the Labor Market After an Interruption in Employment* (Paris: Organization for Economic Cooperation and Development, 1971).

48. Silverberg, Marjorie M. and Eyde, Lorraine D., "Career Part Time Employment: Personnel Implications for the HEW Professional and Executive Corps." National Civil Service League, *Good Government,* Fall 1971.

49. Stewart, C.A., et al., *Job Sharing in Municipal Government: A Case Study in the City of Palo Alto* (Stanford: Stanford University Action Research Liaison Office, 1975).

50. Summers, Clyde W. and Love, Margaret C., "Work Sharing as an Alternative to Layoffs by Seniority: Title VII Remedies in Recession," *University of Pennsylvania Law Review,* April 1976.

51. Temporary Commission on Management and Productivity in the Public Sector, *An Introduction to Alternative Work Schedules and Their Application in the State of New York* (Albany: 1977).

52. U.S. Bureau of Labor Statistics, Special Labor Force Reports, No. 201, "Work Experience of the

Population in 1976" (Washington, D.C.: U.S. Government Printing Office).

53. U.S. Bureau of Labor Statistics, *Handbook of Labor Statistics 1976* (Washington, D.C.: U.S. Government Printing Office, 1977).

54. U.S. Comptroller General, Report to the Congress, *Part-Time Employment in Federal Agencies* FPCD-75-156 (Washington, D.C.: U.S. General Accounting Office, January 2, 1976).

55. U.S. Congress. House of Representatives, Subcommittee on Employee Ethics and Utilization of the Committee on Post Office and Civil Service, *Part-Time Employment and Flexible Work Hours,* Hearings on H.R. 1627, H.R. 2732 and H.R. 2930, 95th Congress, 1st Session, May 24, 26, June 29, July 8, and October 4, 1977.

56. U.S. Congress. House of Representatives, Subcommittee on Manpower and Civil Service of the Committee on Post Office and Civil Service, *Alternate Work Schedules and Part-Time Career Opportunities in Federal Government,* Hearings on H.R. 6350, H.R. 3925, and S. 792, 94th Congress, 1st session, September 29, 30, October 7, 1975.

57. U.S. Congress. Senate Subcommittee on Employment, Poverty and Migratory Labor of the Committee on Labor and Public Welfare, *Changing Patterns of Work in America, 1976,* Hearings, 94th Congress, 2nd session, April 7 and 8, 1976.

58. Van der Dos de Willebois, J.L.J.M., "A Workshop for Married Women in Part-Time Employment: Implications of an Experiment in the Netherlands," *International Labor Review,* December 1967.

59. Werther, William B., Jr., "Minishifts: An Alternative to Overtime," *Personnel Journal,* March 1976.

60. _____, "Part-Timers: Overlooked and Undervalued," *Business Horizons,* February 1975.

61. Wilberson, Margaret, B., *Part-Time Work/Flexible Scheduling* (Berkeley: University of California, Center for Continuing Education of Women, 1975).

62. Wisconsin Legislature, Legislative Council, *Part-Time and Flexible Time Employment,* Staff Brief 76-7 (Madison: 1976).

63. Wisconsin State Bureau of Human Resource Services, "A Demonstration Project to Develop and Test a Job Sharing and Flexible Time Arrangement in Wisconsin Civil Service" (Springfield, Virginia: National Technical Information Service, forthcoming).

64. Work in America Institute, *Alternative Work Patterns: Changing Approaches to Work Scheduling* (Scarsdale: 1976).

Part 3:
The Compressed Workweek

5
Highlights and Conclusions

Compressed workweeks are work schedules in which the usual number of full-time hours are worked in fewer than five days. Examples are the 4-day workweek (four 10-hour days) and the 3-day workweek (three 12-hour days). The use of compressed workweeks increased rapidly beginning in 1971, but it appears now that this growth may have peaked out.

How Widely Are Compressed Workweeks Used?

In 1976, about 1,270,000 workers were on compressed workweeks, or 2.1 percent of all full-time nonfarm wage and salary workers, according to U.S. government statistics. However, this figure is slightly lower than the 1975 figure of 2.2 percent. Just under 60 percent of all compressed workweeks are 4-day workweeks. The 3-day and the 4½-day workweek each accounts for almost 20 percent of all compressed workweeks. They are growing at the expense of 4-day weeks. Compressed workweeks have often been used by local governments (in police departments, for example), in computer operations, and in certain small manufacturing plants. Offices are seldom on compressed workweeks and managers themselves rarely use this alternative.

Many organizations using the compressed workweek limit its use to certain work units instead of using it throughout the organization. About four out of ten users have less than 10 percent of their workers on compressed workweeks.

But three out of ten use the compressed workweek for more than 75 percent of their workers. Plants that use compressed workweeks usually do not operate fewer than five days a week—two or three teams of workers on compressed workweeks make it possible to operate for five or more days at a stretch.

Compressed workweeks are judged by managers to be unsuited to certain areas where full coverage is required at all times—such as shipping and receiving departments, switchboards, maintenance services, and especially where there is contact with customers. Other areas in which the use of compressed workweeks may be difficult are some shift-work operations and work units that have to coordinate their output schedules with other units that are not on compressed workweeks.

Experiences with Compressed Workweeks

Compressed workweeks have several important effects on the organizations that use them. According to the survey responses, the good effects of the compressed workweek are that it:
- Improves employee relations:
  Increases employee morale (in almost all cases).
  Eases employee commuting (for half the cases).
- Improves personnel outcomes:
  Reduces absenteeism (for 71 percent of the users).

Reduces turnover (for 60 percent of the users).

Reduces tardiness (for almost half the users).

Eases recruiting (for two-thirds of the users).

There are also several negative effects that pose challenges to management. For example, the compressed workweek:

- Increases worker fatigue (for over half the users).
- Makes the manager's job harder (for a third of the users).
- Makes internal and external communication harder (for a third of the users).

Coverage and work scheduling are sometimes made more difficult, and sometimes easier, by compressed workweeks.

Many of these reports (two-thirds for some of the effects and one-third for others) are based on in-house data collection and analysis.

An organization's experiences with compressed workweeks depend in part on what kind of organization it is and what type of compressed workweek it uses. Manufacturing firms have better experiences with compressed workweeks than other firms do, especially in terms of productivity, fatigue, and work scheduling effects. Similarly, small firms report better results than large firms do for these effects. Users of the 4-day workweek also report good effects more often than do users of the 3-day week.

What Do Non-Users Think?

Organizations that do not use compressed workweeks are quite negative about them. They expect bad results for productivity, fatigue, coverage of work situations, work scheduling, communication, difficulty of the management job, relationships with customers, and others. They expect good results only for employee morale, commuting, and absenteeism. Differences between the views of users and non-users about the effect of compressed workweeks could stem partly from the misperceptions of non-users; it is more likely, however, that they are caused by differences in work settings that would make

compressed workweeks genuinely less satisfactory for them.

Implementation

The most frequent reason organizations gave for adopting compressed workweeks was to improve employee morale and provide another employee benefit. This reason was mentioned by 62 percent of all the users. And 39 percent cited the aims of increasing productivity and improving production scheduling. Other business advantages—such as reduced costs, reduced turnover, and easier recruiting—were also mentioned, but less frequently.

Several implementation steps were usually taken before compressed workweeks were first adopted. They included holding meetings with managers and employees, reviewing labor laws, discussing plans with other organizations, and instituting a trial program at first. Users who took these implementation steps reported favorable experiences somewhat more often than those who did not, thus indicating the value of proper implementation.

Many firms changed their operating schedule when they adopted compressed workweeks. Over a third of them reduced their days of operation and a third also rearranged their shifts.

In most cases, workers on compressed workweeks were not labor union members. There were some cases of union insistence on overtime pay for hours worked beyond eight in a day—a development that makes compressed workweeks prohibitively expensive. Perhaps more serious, however, is that federal labor law requires such overtime pay.

Problems with Compressed Workweeks

Many users of compressed workweeks reported some problems with it. They were usually problems with work scheduling—such as internal coverage, supervision, interdepartmental coordination, or customer service; or they were employee scheduling problems, such as deciding who works when, or conflicts in personal and commuting schedules. The varied solutions to these problems included staggering days off, letting employees voluntarily work out rotations to ensure coverage, and adding flexitime to aid employees in accommodating their work schedules to their personal schedules.

Compressed Workweek Failures

There have been many failures of compressed workweeks. In this 1977 sample, the failure rate was 28 percent—higher than the failure rates of 23 percent recorded in 1974 (Martin, 1975) and 8 percent in 1971 (Wheeler, Gurman, and Tarnowieski, 1972). However, manufacturing users may be less prone to failure than some other firms.

Probably the basic reason for the failure—and, sometimes, the discontinuation—of compressed workweeks is simply a mismatch in the first place between the work setting and the compressed workweek schedule.

When compressed workweeks fail, they fail quite soon—failures are not caused by deteriorating business results of the compressed workweek over time. For a majority of firms that dropped it, discontinuation occurred before a year's use was up. Continuing users, on the other hand, were long-time users—more than three years of use—in a majority of cases. Favorable experiences of users with compressed workweeks generally held up over time, and problems did not increase (productivity may be an exception). But organizations that discontinued compressed workweeks had quite different experiences from continuing users, particularly in terms of productivity and labor costs, but also in terms of worker fatigue, coverage of work situations, work scheduling, the difficulty of the management job, and relationships with customers. All of these were problems for discontinuers, whereas none except fatigue was really an unfavorable experience for continuing long-term users. Furthermore, these experiences of discontinuers were similar to the expectations of non-users.

The major reasons given for dropping compressed workweeks were scheduling, supervision, coverage, or customer service problems. These reasons were cited by more than half of the discontinuers. Ranking second as reasons for failure were bad productivity experiences and high operating costs. Employee dissatisfaction, too, was sometimes mentioned.

What Is the Future for Compressed Workweeks?

The use of compressed workweeks may have peaked out. Fewer workers were on these schedules in 1976 than in 1975. Very few organizations are planning or evaluating their use. Failures occur quite often.

When compressed workweeks are discontinued, it is usually because they were not suited to the work setting in which they were used. The only effect of compressed workweeks on the organization that may weaken over time and not measure up to expectations in suitable work settings is productivity.

Because of the importance of the correct work setting to the successful use of compressed workweeks, the future growth of compressed workweeks is likely to be quite limited. However, changes in labor law and in collective bargaining agreements that would waive payment of overtime for hours worked beyond eight in a day (perhaps substituting the length of the workweek as the overtime trigger) would permit more use of compressed workweeks.

6

How and Where Compressed Workweeks Are Used

The compressed workweek refers to all schedules in which the usual number of full-time hours are worked in less than five days. It is distinguished from flexitime in that the work hours are set by the employer rather than the employee, and it is distinguished from part-time employment in that full-time hours are worked even though a full week is not worked.

By far the most frequent compressed work-week schedule used by organizations is the 4-day week, accounting for 57 percent of all compressed workweeks in this sample. Both the 3-day week and the 4½-day week were found 18 percent of the time, with the 3½-day week and the alternating 4-day/5-day week occurring very infrequently (see Exhibit 22).

Usage Patterns for Compressed Workweeks

The fact that there are proportionately more compressed workweek employees in some industries and occupations than in others is discussed in the Introduction and is documented by aggregate U.S. data (see U.S. Bureau of Labor Statistics, 1977). In particular, compressed work-weeks are relatively common in local public administration and among service workers; they are relatively scarce in federal and state public administration, mining, manufacturing, and trade industries, and among managers and professionals. Additional patterns of usage emerge from this survey.

Female Employment

Users of compressed workweeks are more likely than non-users to have a high proportion of women in their workforce; 42 percent of the users have a workforce in which over half the employees are female, compared with only 27

Exhibit 22. Number of days in the compressed workweek (percent of all users).

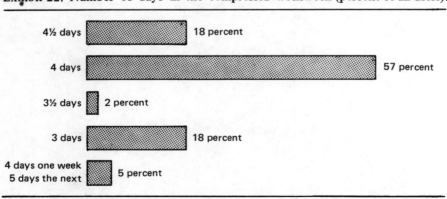

4½ days — 18 percent
4 days — 57 percent
3½ days — 2 percent
3 days — 18 percent
4 days one week 5 days the next — 5 percent

Note: The sample size is 216 uses of compressed workweeks by 155 different organizations.

Exhibit 23. Differences between users and non-users of compressed workweeks, U.S., 1977.

Characteristic	Users (percent)	Non-Users (percent)
Female Employment		
less than 10 percent	7	6
10 to 24 percent	21	25
25 to 50 percent	30	42
more than 50 percent	42	27
Labor Union Membership		
none	66	44
1 to 24 percent	12	17
25 to 75 percent	17	32
more than 75 percent	5	7
Work Technology		
office work	83	90
factory work	63	69
goods produced	39	47
services produced	39	39
heavy strain	17	24
heavy internal communication	50	53
heavy contact with outside suppliers	55	57

Note: Sample size for users is n = 156; for non-users, n = 422.

Exhibit 24. Frequency of use of other alternative work schedules by compressed workweek users and non-users.

Item	Compressed Workweek Users (percent)	Compressed Workweek Non-Users (percent)
Use of Compressed Workweek with Flexitime		
Use flexitime	32	20
Have considered or are planning use of flexitime	29	17
Discontinued flexitime	1	2
Do not use flexitime	38	61
Use of Compressed Workweek with Permanent Part-Time Employment		
Use part-time employment	70	55
Have considered or are planning use of part-time employment	6	6
Discontinued part-time employment	1	1
Do not use part-time employment	23	38

Note: Sample sizes are n=141 compressed workweek users and n=413 compressed workweek non-users. Usage percentages may be used for comparisons but are not valid absolute estimates of usage. See the Introduction and Section 1 of this report and Section 3 and Appendix A of *Part 1: Flexitime* (Nollen and Martin, 1978).

percent of non-users who have this workforce proportion (see Exhibit 23).

Labor Union Membership

Users of compressed workweeks are somewhat less likely than non-users to have substantial labor union representation, as Exhibit 23 shows. Nearly two-thirds of the users had no labor union presence at all, and only 23 percent had as much as a quarter of their workforce represented by unions, compared with 39 percent for non-users where this was the case.

Work Technology

Work technology refers to the nature of a job and what is required to do it (for example, production processes and job requirements) as well as to external demands made on the work unit (for example, relationships with customers and suppliers). Although some work technologies may be better suited to compressed workweeks

than others, no clear relationships emerged in this research. For example, only a slightly smaller number of users than non-users reported that many jobs in their organization involved heavy strain or that there was heavy contact with outside suppliers—despite the fact that these work technologies have been thought unfavorable to compressed workweeks (see Exhibit 23).*

Other Alternative Work Schedules

Users of compressed workweeks are more likely to use other alternative work schedules than are non-users. Both flexitime and permanent part-time employment are found more often in organizations that use compressed workweeks than in those that do not. Thus alternative work schedules appear to complement each

*The measures of work technology are gross measures describing the entire organization, whereas less than half the workforce in a user organization is actually on a compressed workweek, on the average. Thus actual work technology effects may be stronger than revealed in this survey.

Exhibit 25. Operating schedules of compressed workweek users, 1977.

Characteristic	Users (percent)	Non-Users (percent)
Office Operating Schedule (n = 154)		
Hours per day		
eight or fewer	80	96
more than eight	20	4
Shifts per day		
one	95	95
more than one	5	5
Days per week		
fewer than five	19	0
five	78	96
more than five	3	4
Plant Operating Schedule (n = 99)		
Hours per day		
eight or fewer	20	30
more than eight	80	70
Shifts per day		
one	33	26
more than one	67	74
Days per week		
fewer than five	34	0
five	39	64
more than five	27	36

Exhibit 26. Where compressed workweeks are and are not used.

A. *Compressed Workweeks Are Used:*	*Percent of Users*
in individual work units	40
in the manufacturing plant or warehouse	29
in all or nearly all work units, or at headquarters	26
for crews (for example, road maintenance)	5
in the office	5
for exempt employees only	3
for non-exempt employees only	24
for both exempt and non-exempt employees	74
by less than 10 percent of the workers	40
by 10 to 24 percent	11
by 25 to 49 percent	13
by 50 to 75 percent	8
by more than 75 percent	28

B. *Compressed Workweeks Are Not Feasible:*	*Percent of Users*
where customer contact is necessary	20
where regular five-day coverage is necessary (for example, shipping, receiving, switchboard, security, maintenance)	15
for salespeople	12
in the office	11
for shift work on 24-hour operations	8
for work units or jobs that must coordinate output or schedules with other eight-hour units or outside groups	8
for computer operations	7
for managers, high-level administrators, professionals	7
for jobs in which fatigue or strain is a factor	3
for manufacturing	2
where overtime must be paid for more than eight hours a day	1

Note: The average proportion of the workforce on compressed workweeks (among users in this sample) is 35 to 40 percent. The sample size is 151 users in Panel A and 143 responses from 117 users in Panel B. *Exempt employees* refers to workers who are exempt from provisions of the Fair Labor Standards Act—provisions that require payment of overtime premiums for hours worked beyond 40 in a week.

other rather than substitute for each other. (See Exhibit 24.)

Operating Schedule

In this survey, many organizations that used compressed workweeks in their plant operations left their offices on a traditional schedule of eight hours a day and five days a week. Partly because of usage in plant operations, a high proportion of these organizations (80 percent) operated their plants more than eight hours a day. Just over a third of them operated fewer than five days a week (no non-users had short weeks), but the balance operated plants five days or more each week. Thus compressed workweeks (for some or all workers) usually does not imply an idle facility for part of the week (see Exhibit 25).

Where Are Compressed Workweeks Used in the Organization? Where Are They Not Feasible?

In most organizations, compressed workweeks are used in some but not all work units. It is usually not a company-wide practice. Uses in manufacturing plants or warehouses were found among 29 percent of the user organizations, but office uses were infrequent—only 5 percent of all users had compressed workweeks in effect for office operations (see Exhibit 26). The proportion of an organization's workforce on compressed workweeks reflects this usage pattern. Among four out of ten users, less than 10 percent of the workforce was on compressed workweeks. There is, however, a bimodal distribution: More than 75 percent of the workforce was on compressed workweeks among nearly three out of ten users, reflecting cases where most or all of the organization uses this work schedule. The average proportion of a user's workforce on compressed workweeks is 35 to 40 percent, although this average is seldom found because of the bimodal distribution (see Exhibit 26).

The compressed workweek is not feasible as a work schedule where regular five-day coverage is required (unless there are two teams, each with a different day off so that all five days are covered by at least a partial staff). This point was made in about 15 percent of all user responses concerning areas they considered unfeasible for its use. Examples included shipping and receiving departments, the switchboard, maintenance services, and security. But the most common work units where compressed workweeks were believed unworkable were units in which there was customer contact. Of course, these are also areas where five-day coverage or more is usually necessary, but the frame of reference among 20 percent of the responses was customer contact.

Other kinds of work situations thought unsuited to compressed workweeks were office operations (11 percent of all responses), shift work or 24-hour operations (8 percent of all responses), work units or jobs that had to coordinate their output or schedules with other work units (not on compressed workweeks) or with outside groups (8 percent of all responses), jobs in which fatigue or strain is a factor (3 percent of all responses), and manufacturing operations (2 percent of all responses). Particular jobs and work units mentioned for which compressed workweeks might not be possible were sales jobs; management, high-level administrative, and professional jobs; and computer units (12, 7, and 7 percent of all responses, respectively). Only 1 percent of the responses mentioned a need to pay overtime for more than eight hours worked in a day (see Exhibit 26).

7

Effects of Compressed Workweeks on the Organization

Compressed workweeks have a variety of effects on the organizations that use them—effects on workers, on job performance, on management practices, and on a variety of costs. What are these effects? Which are the good effects and which are the bad ones? Are these effects favorable overall?

Experiences of Users of Compressed Workweeks

According to the experiences of 148 user organizations, compressed workweeks have good effects on workers, improve some aspects of job performance but not others, have mixed effects on management, and reduce some costs but leave others unaffected.

Effects on Workers

Improved employee morale is the leading favorable effect of compressed workweeks—almost all users experience it. The effect on employee commuting is also better among over half the users. Thus the extra day off, the reduced number of commuting trips, and off-rush-hour timing of some commuting trips all constitute a payoff for workers (see Exhibit 27).

Effects on Job Performance

Compressed workweeks are likely to reduce turnover and absenteeism (reported by 60 and 71 percent of the users, respectively), but also to worsen fatigue (in 53 percent of the cases). No clear conclusion can be stated for productivity; it was reported to increase by 39 percent of the users and to worsen by just 14 percent, despite increased fatigue (there may be offsetting productivity advantages resulting from reduced turnover, absenteeism, and tardiness and, in some cases, from increased utilization of capital equipment).

Effects on Communication and Management Aspects

If not all employees in an organization are on compressed workweeks, there may be communication problems since not all employees will be present at the same time. In addition to communication, interdepartmental scheduling and coordination may also become more difficult. On the other hand, the longer block of work time permitted by compressed workweeks may aid work coverage and scheduling.

The evidence is that each happens—that no general conclusion can be made, but rather that the result is situation-specific. Most frequently, however, there is no effect of compressed workweeks on communication or management aspects. In particular, coverage of work situations, employee scheduling, and work scheduling are each aided among 20 to 30 percent of the users and hindered for a similar number—but unaffected for roughly half the users. Communication and the overall difficulty of the management job are made more difficult by compressed workweeks for a third of the users, but are unaffected more than half the time. Nevertheless, these latter two features are the most frequently reported bad effects of compressed workweeks (see Exhibits 27 and 28).

Effects on Costs

For a substantial number of organizations that use compressed workweeks (four out of ten),

overtime costs are reduced, in turn reducing unit labor costs. A regular ten-hour shift under a compressed workweek schedule, for example, is likely to have lower labor costs than is a regular eight-hour shift with two hours of overtime. Utilities costs are reduced for 35 percent of the users of compressed workweeks (obviously the case where the plant closes on the fifth day). Recruiting costs and effort are reduced for most users—a reduction consistent with the reduced turnover attributed to compressed workweeks (see Exhibit 27).

Exhibit 27. Effects of compressed workweeks on the organization: the experiences of 148 users.

Nature of Effects	Changes Attributed to Compressed Workweeks (percent of all users)		
	Better	No Change	Worse
Effects on Employees			
Employee morale	90	9	1
Employee commuting	54	34	12
Effects on Job Performance			
Productivity	39	47	14
Turnover	60	38	2
Absenteeism	71	27	2
Tardiness	46	45	9
Fatigue	9	39	53
Effects on Communication			
Internal communication	9	59	32
External communication	8	61	31
Effects on Management Aspects			
Coverage of work situations	28	42	30
Employee scheduling	20	53	28
Work scheduling	28	48	25
Difficulty of management job	11	54	34
Effects on Costs			
Unit labor costs	36	56	8
Overtime costs	40	49	11
Personnel administration costs	11	76	13
Training costs	9	80	11
Recruiting	69	28	3
Utilities costs	35	52	12
Support services costs	19	70	11
Effects on Customers, Suppliers and the Public			
Effects on customers	10	72	18
Effects on suppliers	3	85	12
Public relations	38	55	7

Exhibit 28. The good and bad effects of compressed workweeks: the experiences of 148 users, U.S., 1977[a]

Good Effects[b]	Bad Effects[c]	Effects Sometimes Good, Sometimes Bad[d]
Improves employee morale	Increases fatigue	Coverage of work situations
Reduces absenteeism	Increases difficulty of management job	Work scheduling
Eases recruiting	Worsens internal communication	Employee scheduling
Reduces turnover	Worsens external communication	
Eases employee commuting		
Reduces tardiness		

Notes:

[a]In approximate order from strongest to weakest.

[b]Half or more of all users reported better results attributed to compressed workweeks, with few or no worse results reported.

[c]One-third or more of all users reported worse results attributed to compressed workweeks, with few better results reported.

[d]About an even split between better and worse results attributed to compressed workweeks, with many no-change results also.

Effects on Customers, Suppliers, and the Public

Users of compressed workweeks do not experience bad effects on customers or suppliers. This most likely occurs because they are not used in areas where five-day customer contact or supplier contact is necessary—otherwise there would be such a problem.

How Are Effects of Compressed Workweeks Measured?

How do managers know about the effects of compressed workweeks on their organizations? Do they collect data and do in-house surveys or do they base their reported effects on managerial observation? (Of course, not all the effects of

Exhibit 29. Measurement of effects of compressed workweeks.

Effect	Percent of Users Who Collected Data
Effects That Are Often Measured by Data	
Productivity	66
Absenteeism	66
Turnover	63
Employee morale	61
Overtime costs	58
Tardiness	57
Effects That Are Sometimes Measured by Data	
Unit labor costs of production	44
Fatigue	42
Difficulty of management job	36
Effect on customers	36
Employee commuting	33
Recruiting	33
Utilities costs	32

Notes: The sample size is 148 users of compressed workweeks. Data collection is, for example, by organizational survey or analysis of in-house personnel records.

compressed workweeks—such as effects on coverage, communications, or scheduling—are readily measurable in any rigorous or quantitative way.)

Several key good effects of compressed workweeks are measured by data in a majority of the cases. (See Exhibit 29.) Key bad effects are also measured in a substantial number of cases. Effects on job performance and on workers are frequently measured. Thus the results reported for these effects are at least partially documented and not just casual impressions.

Patterns of data collection also reveal which effects of compressed workweeks are important to managers. Aside from job performance and effects on workers, three cost factors are sometimes measured—overtime costs, unit labor costs, and utilities costs. In addition, a key management aspect—the overall difficulty of the management job—is sometimes measured (by more than a third of the users) despite the apparent difficulty of doing so.

Analysis of Experiences with Compressed Workweeks: Does Industry, Size of Firm, or Model Made a Difference?

Compressed workweeks are used in a variety of work settings—in different industries and work technologies, and in small as well as large organizations. It may be schedules as a 4-day week or as a 3-day or 3½-day week. Some user experiences with compressed workweeks may depend on their industrial and size characteristics, and they may depend on which compressed workweek model is used. If they do, better guidance can be given to prospective users on the experiences they might expect.

Industry

Compared with most other industries, the manufacturing industry makes little use of compressed workweeks—yet some outstanding applications of compressed workweeks are found in production facilities. This sample represented a substantial number of manufacturing firms, so a comparison of key effects is possible. In particular, some effects of compressed workweeks that might theoretically be expected to differ

for manufacturing firms compared with other firms are productivity, fatigue, communication, work scheduling, difficulty of the management job, labor costs, and relationships with suppliers and customers.

Another way to investigate how these effects vary with the work setting is to compare results for goods producers versus services producers. (These comparisons are quite rough and must remain tentative because of small sample sizes for these categories and because usually not all workers in an organization are on compressed workweeks—thus allowing for the possibility that a manufacturing firm would not have production workers on compressed workweeks.)

For most of the effects of compressed workweeks where industry might make a difference, manufacturing firms have better experiences than do firms in finance and insurance, and goods producers have better experiences than services producers do (the finance and insurance industry was chosen for analysis because production processes in that industry are much different from those in manufacturing and because there was a large enough sample size). For example, users in both manufacturing and goods producing are more likely to report better productivity than are their counterparts in finance and insurance or in services production. These results may be traced to the reduced number of start-ups and shut-downs and the better utilization of capital equipment provided by compressed workweeks—factors that are especially important to manufacturing firms. Consistent with these productivity results is the lessened incidence of fatigue problems in manufacturing—less fatigue should also mean higher productivity (see Exhibit 30).

Another difference between manufacturing users and finance and insurance users is that work scheduling is less likely to be affected (made neither harder nor easier) for the former. In other areas—such as communication, difficulty of the management job, unit labor costs, and relationships with customers—manufacturing users and goods producers also show a slightly higher frequency of favorable experiences than other users do, but the differences are not statistically significant.

Exhibit 30. Differences in effects of compressed workweeks by industry.

	Industry	
Effect	Manufacturing	Finance, Insurance
Productivity (percent reporting better)	44	26
Fatigue (percent reporting worse)	42	64
Work scheduling (percent reporting better)	22	31
(percent reporting no change)	54	38
(percent reporting worse)	24	33
Internal communications (percent reporting worse)	30	31
Difficulty of management job (percent reporting worse)	31	34
Unit labor costs (percent reporting better)	35	28
Relationship with suppliers (percent reporting worse)	11	9
Relationship with customers (percent reporting worse)	14	23

	Producers of	
Effect	Goods	Services
Productivity (percent reporting better)	46	38
Fatigue (percent reporting worse)	38	59
Work scheduling (percent reporting better)	20	42
(percent reporting no change)	46	33
(percent reporting worse)	24	25
Internal communications (percent reporting worse)	28	31
Difficulty of management job (percent reporting worse)	30	37
Unit labor costs (percent reporting better)	44	42
Relationship with suppliers (percent reporting worse)	14	13
Relationship with customers (percent reporting worse)	16	22

Notes: Sample sizes are n=67 for manufacturing, n=39 for finance and insurance, n=60 for goods producers, and n=55 for services producers. Differences across industries for productivity, fatigue, and work scheduling (no change) are statistically significant.

These results mean that failure to use compressed workweeks by manufacturing firms cannot be attributed to the prospect of bad experiences—because when they do use compressed workweeks, their experiences are better than average. This does not imply, however, that all manufacturing firms can successfully use compressed workweeks. There will of course be production situations that do not allow it, or external influences such as labor law or trade union opposition that prevent it.

Size of Firm

In a few key effects of compressed workweeks on the organization, small firms reported favorable experiences more often than large firms. For example, over half the small firms (fewer

Exhibit 31. Differences in effects of compressed workweeks in small versus large firms.

Effect	Size of Firm	
	Small ⩽500 employees	Large >1000 employees
Productivity (percent reporting better)	54	27
Work scheduling (percent reporting better)	27	31
(percent reporting no change)	61	40
(percent reporting worse)	12	30
Internal communications (percent reporting worse)	39	34
Difficulty of management job (percent reporting worse)	27	39
Unit labor costs (percent reporting better)	42	33

Notes: Sample sizes are n=62 for small firms and n=71 for large firms. Differences across firm sizes for productivity and work scheduling are statistically significant.

than 500 employees) reported improved productivity, but only a quarter of the large firms (more than 1,000 employees) did so. Work scheduling was seldom a problem in small firms, though it was worsened in 30 percent of the large firms. There were also small advantages for small firms in terms of unit labor costs and the difficulty of the management job (see Exhibit 31).

4-Day Versus 3-Day Weeks

Compressed workweeks reported on in this study include 3-day and 3½-day weeks as well as 4-day and 4½-day weeks. Because 3-day weeks ordinarily mean a longer day and a different work schedule for the unit using this schedule than does the more common 4-day week, some effects of 3-day weeks may differ from those

Exhibit 32. Effects of the 4-day versus the 3-day workweek.

Effect		Compressed Workweek Model	
		4-Day Week	3-Day Week
Productivity	(percent reporting better)	42	23
	(percent reporting worse)	34	57
Fatigue	(percent reporting worse)	57	71
	(percent reporting better)	31	34
Work scheduling	(percent reporting no change)	47	37
	(percent reporting worse)	22	29
Internal communications (percent reporting worse)		23	46
Difficulty of management job (percent reporting worse)		31	32
Unit labor costs (percent reporting better)		40	38
Utilities costs (percent reporting better)		46	14
Employee morale (percent reporting better)		91	94

Notes: Sample sizes are n=83 for a 4-day week and n=35 for 3-day week (includes four users with a 3½-day week). Differences across models are statistically significant for productivity, fatigue, internal communications, and utilities costs.

Exhibit 33. Expectations of 365 non-users of the effects of compressed work-weeks.

Nature of Effects	Expected Changes Attributed to Compressed Workweeks (percent of all non-users)		
	Better	No Change	Worse
Effects on Employees			
Employee morale	66	24	11
Employee commuting	51	31	19
Effects on Job Performance			
Productivity	21	32	48
Turnover	41	43	16
Absenteeism	57	28	16
Tardiness	28	50	23
Fatigue	7	12	81
Effects on Communication			
Internal communication	5	52	43
External communication	3	41	56
Effects on Management Aspects			
Coverage of work situations	10	26	65
Employee scheduling	10	29	61
Work scheduling	11	26	63
Difficulty of management job	4	34	62
Effects on Costs			
Unit labor costs	17	46	38
Overtime costs	22	39	39
Personnel administration costs	5	60	35
Training costs	6	75	19
Recruiting	47	39	14
Utilities costs	36	43	21
Support services costs	23	51	26
Effects on Customers, Suppliers, and the Public			
Effects on customers	4	38	58
Effects on suppliers	2	60	38
Public relations	30	55	15

of 4-day weeks. These results are presented for each compressed workweek model separately in Exhibit 32. (Because the number of users of 3-day weeks in this sample is quite small—n=35—the conclusions to follow should be regarded as tentative.)

Overall, 4-day workweeks give better results than do 3-day workweeks. Productivity is more likely to be better for those on 4-day weeks than for those on 3-day weeks. Indeed, productivity is a problem with 3-day weeks; 57 percent of 3-day week users reported worse productivity. Similarly, fatigue is a common problem with 3-day weekers—71 percent of all 3-day weekers experienced worse fatigue. Work scheduling is more likely to be affected under 3-day weeks, and internal communication is more likely to be worsened. Utilities costs are seldom reduced under 3-day weeks, whereas there are savings among almost half the 4-day weekers. All these results are no doubt traceable to the need to coordinate 3-day workers with other operations spanning five or more days, while 4-day operations are more likely to be self-contained with shutdowns on the fifth day. The 3-day week is usually confined to certain work units—for example, the electronic data processing department.

Expectations of Non-Users

It is to be expected that the experiences of users of compressed workweeks would on balance be favorable—otherwise they would not persist in its use. But what about employers who do not use compressed workweeks? Do they have generally unfavorable expectations of its effects? Do they see some potentially good experiences?

Overall, organizations that do not use (have never used) compressed workweeks are quite negative about them. They foresee only three strongly positive effects: employee morale, commuting, and absenteeism. They expect bad results in terms of productivity, worker fatigue, coverage of work situations, employee scheduling, work scheduling, difficulty of the management job, and relationships with customers and suppliers (see Exhibit 33).

Users and non-users of compressed workweeks are in agreement only on its effects on employee commuting, internal communication, and utilities costs. In other respects, non-users have a considerably dimmer view. Of course, these results could arise from differences between user and non-user characteristics that would make compressed workweeks less suitable for organizations that do not now use them. For example, many non-users who would expect worse relations with customers because of compressed workweeks (even though current users seldom report such experiences) may have operations in which customers would genuinely be adversely affected if compressed workweeks were adopted. Users, on the other hand, may not have such operations, so they can use compressed workweeks without bad effects. Since there were more non-users than users in the manufacturing industry (for which somewhat better results were reported), and there was little difference in the size distribution of users versus non-users, differences between users' experiences and non-users' expectations cannot be explained on those accounts.

In sum, prospects for the expansion of the compressed workweek through its adoption by current non-users are in doubt. While some of the negative views held by non-users may be simple misperceptions (for example, overestimation of fatigue problems), their other doubts may be justified by the nature of their operations that would make compressed workweeks unsuitable. Collective bargaining agreements and wage and hour law continue to be a restraint (see the following Section).

8
Managing Compressed Workweeks

Compressed workweeks quite frequently pose new challenges to management and make the manager's job more difficult. In some cases, they complicate scheduling and coverage, but in other cases they make it easier. In this section, attention is focused on the successful management of compressed workweeks: where they originate, why they are used, how they are implemented, what accompanying schedule changes are made, what the role of labor unions is, and what problems are encountered and how they are solved.

Why Are Compressed Workweeks Implemented?

The suggestion to use compressed workweeks usually originated with top management (51 percent of all users), or with personnel or personnel-related departments (23 percent of all users). (It should be noted that respondents themselves were personnel executives or other top managers.) Employees requested compressed workweeks in 16 percent of the cases.

Why do managers adopt compressed workweeks? Various good effects attributed to compressed workweeks have been noted—improved employee morale, reduced absenteeism, easier recruiting, reduced turnover, easier employee commuting, and reduced tardiness, to name the leading good effects (see the preceding section). However, a reported good effect may or may not be important to the employer and hence

may or may not be decisive in explaining its use. When employers were asked the open-ended question, "Why do you use compressed workweeks?" the answers were of two types: reasons focused on employees, and reasons focused on the organization.

The more frequently offered single reasons for using compressed workweeks were to improve employee morale and to improve productivity or production scheduling—offered respectively by 44 percent and 39 percent of the users. Improving turnover, absenteeism, tardiness, and recruiting were indicated as usage reasons by 21 percent of the organizations (see Exhibit 34).

These same reasons also are among the leading good *effects* reported by these users of compressed workweeks—except for productivity. Although it was a positive experience more often than negative, it did not emerge as a strong plus for compressed workweeks. Thus it appears that employers are achieving their goals with compressed workweeks except for the productivity goal.

In managers' own words, the benefits to employees are perceived as follows:

- "Gives employees more continuous free time, and therefore they may approach the workweek with a more positive attitude" (from a small midwestern company in communications/publishing).
- "More uninterrupted leisure time" (from a

medium-size industrial manufacturing company in the Midwest).

- "Employees have more personal time for further education or other part-time work" (from a large eastern manufacturing company).
- "Fewer workdays mean reduced transportation time and expense" (from a medium-size industrial manufacturing company in the Midwest).

Benefits to the organization were also described by managers:

- "Provides longer, more productive days on travelling work crews" (from a large western state government).
- "Solves an operating problem involving mid-week work load peak" (from a large bank on the West Coast).
- "Allows scheduling more police officers at peak workload hours" (from a small midwestern municipal police department).
- "You can provide extended coverage for a position without having to pay overtime premium or setting up second shifts with undesirable hours" (from a large eastern life insurance company).
- "Two three-day week operations provide Saturday coverage without premium (one operation Mon. Tues. Wed.—one operation Thurs. Fri. Sat.)" (from a large diversified company based in the Midwest).
- "Allows maximum time on project work. Less start-up and shut-down time" (from a moderately large financial institution in the Midwest).
- "Reduced requests for time off for personal reasons" (from a large midwestern telephone company).
- "It has helped us attract employees with greater potential within the labor market" (from a moderately large manufacturing company in the Midwest).

Implementation Steps

The list of implementation steps that can be taken once the idea of compressed workweeks is raised is long and varied, ranging from discussing compressed workweek plans with other organizations to documenting the quantitative results of a pilot program. The implementation steps can be broken down into a planning phase and adoption phase. The planning phase includes all fact-finding and opinion-gathering steps and identification of internal management responsibilities. The adoption phase includes changes instituted in organizations because of compressed workweeks as well as its actual start-up and the possible measurement of results.

Exhibit 34. Reasons for using compressed workweeks.

Reason	Percent of All Users
Improve employee morale and satisfaction; improve employee relations; convenience to employees	44
Provide an additional employee benefit; give employees another day off	18
Increase productivity, improve production scheduling, increase capital utilization	39
Reduce costs; less overtime, overhead	14
Make recruiting easier, higher quality people available, make shift-work more attractive	11
Decrease absenteeism, turnover, tardiness	10
Provide better service, stay open longer hours	7
Other	5

Notes: The sample size is 147. Percent total exceeds 100 because of multiple responses.

Exhibit 35. Implementation steps taken by users of compressed workweeks.

Implementation Steps	Percent of All Users
Planning Phase	
Held meetings with managers, supervisors	70
Held meetings with employees	66
Reviewed state and federal labor laws	52
Discussed plan with other organizations	48
Appointed an internal project director	13
Held meetings with union representatives	10
An organization member attended a seminar or conference	9
Engaged an outside consultant	1
Adoption Phase	
Instituted first on trial basis	68
Employees voted on adoption	26
Provided for audit of results	26
Established baseline data for formal evaluation of	
— business results	26
— employee attitudes	23
Work restructured	20
Employee cross-trained	9

Notes: The sample size is 150 users of compressed workweeks. Totals exceed 100 percent because of multiple responses.

In this sample of users, four implementation steps were often taken in the planning phase: meetings were held with managers, supervisors, and employees; state and federal labor laws were reviewed (indicating widespread awareness of their sometimes constraining effects); and the ideas were discussed with other organizations. More newsworthy are the steps that were usually not taken: an internal project director was appointed by only one user out of five, and attendance at outside conferences or use of consultants was rare. Union representatives were consulted in most cases where there was a labor union presence (see Exhibit 35).

In the adoption phase, a trial program was usually used first. But other implementation steps were taken much less frequently. Measurement of results, for example, was taken by roughly only one in four users. Work was restructured to accommodate compressed workweeks by 20 percent of the users.

If the implementation steps taken by a large number of users are really important, they should be associated with an improvement in their experiences with compressed workweeks compared with those of users who do not take these steps. A few key effects of compressed workweeks were checked separately for users who did and who did not hold meetings with managers and supervisors and with employees (the most common steps in the planning phase of implementation), and who did and did not institute compressed workweeks first on a trial basis (the only common implementation step in the adoption phase). The effects checked were controversial job performance, management, and cost variables: productivity, work scheduling internal communication, the difficulty of the management job, and unit labor costs.

The results? In almost all cases, these experiences with compressed workweeks were more likely to be favorable when the common implementation steps were undertaken than when they were not. In particular, holding meetings with managers and supervisors was associated with better productivity and work scheduling experiences, with improved labor costs and, as expected, with a lower frequency of management

Exhibit 36. Implementation steps that improve key experiences with compressed workweeks.

Experience with	Held Meetings With Mgrs., Suprs.		Held Meetings With Employees		Instituted First on a Trial Basis	
	Yes	No	Yes	No	Yes	No
Productivity						
percent reporting better	43	28	42	31	41	33
percent reporting worse	9	26	10	22	9	26
Work Scheduling						
percent reporting better	32	16	31	20	no effect	
percent reporting worse	19	39	18	38		
Internal Communication						
percent reporting worse	no effect		29	36	27	40
Difficulty of the Management Job						
percent reporting worse	31	43	no effect		14	62
Unit Labor Costs						
percent reporting better	42	23	43	23	37	33

Notes: Sample sizes are n=105 and n=43 for those who did and did not hold meetings with managers and supervisors, n=102 and n=45 for those who did and did not hold meetings with employees, and n=99 and n=49 for those who did and did not institute first on a trial basis.

Exhibit 37. Changes in operating schedule brought about by adoption of compressed workweeks.

Change	Percent of All Users
Operate fewer days per week	38
Operate more days per week	13
Operate same number of days per week but with staggered days off for employees working compressed schedules	48
Rearranged shifts	36
Other changes	13

Notes: The sample size is 150 users of compressed workweeks. The total exceeds 100 percent because of multiple responses.

Exhibit 38. Labor union membership among 150 compressed workweek users.

Degree of Union Membership	Percent of All Users
Less than 10 percent	84
10 to 49 percent	3
50 to 75 percent	5
More than 75 percent	9

problems. The other implementation steps brought about similar good results (see Exhibit 36). Of course, there is no guarantee that any single implementation step will yield superior experiences with compressed workweeks; the results reported are merely simple associations. However, the associations are not likely to be merely the result of a Hawthorne effect—a short-lived phenomenon caused just by doing something—because most of the users of compressed workweeks are relatively long-term users (see the preceding Section). Although there is no documentation of the mechanism by which these implementation steps work, the results are likely to be real and enduring.

Changes in Operating Schedule

When compressed workweeks were introduced, many organizations made changes in their operating schedules. About 38 percent of them reduced their days of operation (for example, closing the plant on the fifth day). Some users (19 percent) operated more days (for example, by adding Saturday operations and scheduling a Thursday-Saturday as well as a Monday-Wednesday team in a 3-day compressed workweek for each team). More than a third of the users rearranged shifts (see Exhibit 37).

Shift changes were of many varieties. For the 4-day week combined with 5-day operation, the simplest change is dividing the workforce into two teams, each working four days—a Monday-Thursday team and a Tuesday-Friday team. This staggering of workers keeps all functions at least partially covered during all five days. In 4-day operations with two shifts, hours may be re-arranged; for example, if the old hours were 7:00 a.m. to 3:30 p.m. and 4:00 p.m. to 12:30 a.m., the new hours might be 6:00 a.m. to 4:00 p.m. and 4:00 p.m. to 2:00 a.m. A respondent who reported this shift change also altered the old holiday plan of ten paid holidays (eight hours each) to eight paid holidays (ten hours each).

In computer operations, two 12-hour shifts a day for two teams of workers each working three days (one on Monday-Wednesday and the other on Thursday-Saturday) is a way to achieve six-day coverage 24 hours a day.

Peak workloads during one part of the day or week can also be managed through certain shift arrangements. In police work, for example, ten-hour shifts can be overlapped: a 7:00 a.m. to 5:00 p.m. shift, a 5:00 p.m. to 3:00 a.m. shift, and a third 9:00 p.m. to 7:00 a.m. shift overlapping the busy night hours. Overloaded areas in a firm's operation can be eased by adding a Friday-Sunday team in those areas, thus adding weekend hours, or a weekend team can replace a third weekday shift. Compressed workweeks that are 4½ days long are often accomplished by adding an hour a day to Monday-Thursday operations to permit Friday afternoons off.

Changes in Compressed Workweek Model

About one in four users of compressed workweeks changed the way in which they originally used it. Some of these changes were to extend a 4½-day week from summer months to more months in the year; some changes were to reduce the hours in the workweek; and some changes were to switch from a 4-day to a 3-day week.

The Role of Labor Unions

The influence of labor unions on the use of compressed workweeks is sometimes positive and sometimes negative. In most organizations using compressed workweeks, there was little or no labor union representation (see Exhibit 38). Among compressed workweek employees themselves, there was even less union membership— few or no union members in 84 percent of the cases. But in about one user organization out of seven in this sample, half or more of the compressed workweek employees were union members.

The chief negative union influence on the use of compressed workweeks is that some unions insist on overtime pay at time-and-a-half for all hours worked beyond eight in a single day, thus making compressed workweeks prohibitively costly to management. However, in several cases among this sample of users, labor unions willingly agreed to change overtime provisions to begin after 10 or 12 hours a day, whichever the altered regular day length was. Occasionally, locals favored compressed workweeks despite opposition by the national or international union. The overtime problem, of course, is not solely a creation of some labor unions. Federal labor law requires some employers to make overtime payments after eight hours. Even where unions favor compressed workweeks, management is sometimes hesitant, fearing that a four-day, ten-hour-a-day schedule will turn into a four-day, eight-hour-a-day schedule under union pressure without any reduction in pay—thus ending up as a reduction in total working time.

Problems and Solutions

A large majority of continuing users of compressed workweeks (over 60 percent) reported at least one problem with its use. (See Exhibit 39.) Most of the time the problems are either work scheduling or employee scheduling problems. Work scheduling problems include problems of internal coverage, supervision, or interdepartmental coordination; problems of customer service or supplier contact; and problems of communication. Employee scheduling problems include problems of deciding who works when, conflicts with home and family life, and prob-

Exhibit 39. Problems encountered in the use of compressed workweeks.

Problem	Percent of 115 Responses
Work scheduling problems	38
internal coverage, supervision, or coordination problems	22
customer service or supplier problems	12
communications problems	4
Employee scheduling problems	26
weekend staffing, setting shift hours, or deciding who works compressed schedules	15
employee home and family life problems, commuting problems	11
Fringe benefit reallocation—vacation, sick leave time	11
Overtime—how to avoid it equitably	9
Fatigue	6
Other (including employees who don't know what to do with extra time off)	9

lems with commuting schedules. Together, these problems account for two-thirds of all the problems mentioned.

Exhibit 40. Examples of problems with compressed workweeks and their solutions (actual reports from users).

Problem	Solution
Work scheduling problems	
Poor supervisory coverage.	Asked supervisors to work five days.
Coverage in all departments was necessary at all times.	Maintained skeleton crews and compensatory time off was granted.
Telephone coverage, Friday billing.	Cross-training; some people work five days (eight hours a day).
Customer service coverage on Friday afternoons.	Group established its own rotating coverage so a person would be present.
Customer service calls.	Rearranged shifts.
Incoming freight.	Notified local delivering carriers.
Maintaining contact with distributors, salesmen on Fridays.	Scheduled necessary contact employees on a Tuesday-Friday workweek.

Exhibit 40 (continued).

Problem	Solution

Work scheduling problems (cont.)

Problem of service to policyholders.	Assigned 7 percent of 4-day workweek force to a Tuesday-Friday schedule with 93 percent working Monday-Thursday.
Supervisors did not like to work Friday afternoon.	We found that neither policyowners nor agents came in or called on Friday so we use an answering service for all closed hours.
Communication from one team to another.	We developed a one-hour overlap.
Communications with employees much more complex.	Required added management time.

Employee scheduling problems

Starting times for employees under flexitime schedule were not acceptable when the ten-hour workday was instituted.	Employees were permitted to select a new flexitime schedule; lunch hours were cut to 30 minutes to shorten the day.
Office employees who contact customers also wanted a 4-day week.	We staggered their workweek; that is, half had Monday off, half Friday.
Too many wanted Mondays or Fridays off.	Each department's management simply spelled out the minimum staff required for those days and it was left up to work groups to decide who would be there.
Adverse effect on nonparticipating employees' morale.	Not solved.
Some married women with children find it inconvenient to arrive home late.	Solved by putting only those people who want the 4-day week in that department.
Changing of daily shift hours.	Employees had to adjust and in some cases change their transportation.
Train schedules for departing employees require up to 1½ hr. wait on Friday afternoon.	Called Burlington Railroad—they are adding a train.
Babysitting and transportation.	Allowed flexibility in reporting and quitting times.

Fringe benefit reallocation problems

How to pay for benefits such as days of vacation, holidays, funeral pay, sick days.	Generally we divided by "4" instead of "5." Everyone involved gets "1" less, but the same number of hours.
Sick days.	Had to change "sick days" to "sick hours" because of longer working day in 4-day week. Now give 48 hours per year instead of six days.

Exhibit 40 (continued).

Problem	*Solution*
Overtime problems	
We are covered by federal law requiring overtime after eight hours.	Restructured wage schedule was developed to yield equal pay under new and old schedule.
Walsh-Healy Act requires overtime for hours over eight in a day for all work on government contract.	We dropped U.S. Government as customers.
Due to Walsh-Healy, having to pay overtime for over eight hours worked.	Not solved and is why we have not expanded use of compressed workweeks.

Solutions to these problems are varied. Often, coverage is achieved by staggering days off (some have Friday off and others have Monday off). Often, too, employees themselves work out rotations to ensure coverage. Communication problems were sometimes solved by overlapping teams by an hour. Some employees under a compressed workweek who found their working hours inconvenient were offered flexible working hours along with their compressed workweek.

Fringe benefit problems usually involved questions of how to handle holiday or sick leave. The most frequent answer was to express these leaves in terms of hours rather than days. For example, the former six sick-leave days (amounting to 48 hours) were converted to 48 hours of sick leave under compressed workweeks (amounting to 4.8 days a year in a 4-day workweek or four days a year in a 3-day workweek).

Overtime problems were encountered in cases where time-and-a-half was required by law or union agreement to be paid for all hours worked beyond eight in a day. For some organizations, this problem blocked the use of compressed workweeks in certain areas. An innovative solution to the overtime problem was to pay overtime for, say, the ninth and tenth hours each day but also to reduce the basic wage rate to leave daily earnings the same as before. (See Exhibit 40 for examples of problems with compressed workweeks and accompanying solutions, expressed in managers' own words). See Appendix B of *Part 1: Flexitime* — Nollen and Martin, 1978 — for a discussion of labor law affecting alternative work schedules, including compressed workweeks.

9

The Future of the Compressed Workweek

After a spectacular increase in popularity in the early 1970's—going from a handful of workers in 1971 to over 1,330,000 workers in 1975—compressed workweeks may have peaked out. There were actually fewer workers on these schedules in 1976 than in 1975 (no comparative data are yet available for 1977). A substantial number of organizations in this survey that once used compressed workweeks have discontinued them—numbering more than one out of every four one-time users. Only 2 percent of all respondents were currently planning or evaluating the use of compressed workweeks in 1977. By contrast, 23 percent of the respondents to a 1971 American

Exhibit 41. Failure rates for compressed workweeks.

Failure Rate (percent)	Year	Study	Sample Size	Sample Characteristics
28	1977	Nollen and Martin (1978)	215	All industries, but especially manufacturing, and finance and insurance; all compressed workweek models, but majority 4-day workweek.
23	1974	Martin (1975)	66	All industries, but especially manufacturing and services; few large firms; all compressed workweek models, but mainly 4-day workweek.
23	1974	Weinstein (1975)	69	Mainly manufacturing firms; mostly small firms; mostly 4-day workweek.
8	1971	Wheeler, Gurman, and Tarnowieski (1972)	156	Mostly manufacturing firms; many small firms; 4-day workweek only.

Note: Three other studies reported failure rates but were based on very small sample sizes. See text.

Exhibit 42. Failure rates for compressed workweeks by industry and plant operating schedule.

Characteristic	Failure Rate (percent)
Industry	
Manufacturing (n=89)	23
Finance and insurance (n=51)	22
All other industries (n=54)	46
Plant operating schedule	
Plant shifts	
one per day (n=42)	21
more than one per day (n=96)	31

Management Association's survey were planning or evaluating a 4-day week (Wheeler, Gurman, and Tarnowieski, 1972).

What are the future prospects for compressed workweeks? Which organizations discontinue them? Is the failure rate getting higher? Why do they sometimes fail? Do users' experiences with compressed workweeks become less favorable with longer duration of use? Why do non-users decide against adopting compressed workweeks?

Compressed Workweek Failures

The failure rate for compressed workweeks as of 1977 recorded from this sample was 28 percent—59 discontinuers out of a total of 215 one-time users. This figure is somewhat higher than the 23 percent failure rates found in 1974 by both Martin (from a total sample of 66) and Weinstein (from a total sample of 69) and much worse than the 8 percent failure rate recorded in 1971 from a total sample of 156 by Wheeler, Gurman, and Tarnowieski (see Exhibit 41). High failure rates have also been reported by two other studies in recent years: A 44 percent failure rate found in 1975 by Haldi and a 40 percent failure rate reported by the Comptroller General (1975). An early study by Poor (1970) reported a 19 percent failure rate. Sample sizes in these studies were quite small, however—23 in Haldi, 15 in Comptroller General, and 17 in Poor.

Who Discontinues Compressed Workweeks?

Is there any relationship between certain characteristics of organizations and the fact that they discontinued their use of compressed workweeks? Are these organizations different from others that continue its use? The answers are that organizational size does not seem to matter, but that the particular industry and the plant operating schedule involved may matter. The failure rate among manufacturing users of compressed workweeks in this survey was 23 percent. Among users in the finance and insurance industry it was 22 percent. Both of these failure rates were lower than those among users in other industries. In addition, organizations with more than one shift in plant operations may have been more frequent discontinuers, perhaps because of the increased scheduling and coordination problems involved in multiple shifts (see Exhibit 42).

Why Do Compressed Workweeks Fail?

There are two leading hypotheses to explain why compressed workweeks are discontinued in some organizations. The first is that its effects on the organization become unfavorable after longer duration of use—that good experiences weaken and problems grow. The second is that compressed workweeks are unsuited to the work setting among firms that discontinue it—that it was a mistake to use compressed workweeks in the first place.

Exhibit 43. Duration of use of compressed workweeks by discontinuers and by continuing users.

Duration of Use	Percent of Organizations
By organizations that discontinued use	
Less than six months	27
Six months to one year	32
One to two years	27
Two to three years	10
More than three years	4
By continuing users	
Less than six months	11
Six months to one year	9
One to two years	7
Two to three years	16
More than three years	57

Notes: The sample sizes are 41 discontinuers and 150 continuing users. The average duration of use was three to four years.

In order to learn why compressed workweeks fail, the following questions are posed: How long did organizations use compressed workweeks before they dropped them? Are the experiences of long-term users less favorable than the experiences of short-term users? Are experiences reported in 1977 in this study less favorable than experiences reported in 1974 and 1971 by previous studies? How are the experiences reported by discontinuers different from the experiences reported by continuing users in this study? What reasons do discontinuers give for dropping compressed workweeks?

Duration of Use

Organizations that discontinued their use of compressed workweeks made this decision quite soon—59 percent had dropped it before a year was up. Only 14 percent carried compressed workweeks as long as two years before dropping it. On the other hand, continuing users were by and large long-term users—over half of them had used compressed workweeks for more than three years, and nearly three-quarters had passed the two-year mark (see Exhibit 43). These results indicate that failures show up quickly, as would be the case in mismatches between the work schedule and the work setting. They also suggest that successful implementations continue to be successful, without serious bad results developing later on.

Experiences over Time

To extend these results, users' experiences with compressed workweeks over time can be analyzed. This was done in two ways: by com-

Exhibit 44. Effects of compressed workweeks over time.

Item	Data Source	
	Short-Term vs. Long-Term Users	Longitudinal Comparison
What happens to favorable effects over time?		
Employee morale	no change	n.a.
Employee commuting	strengthens	strengthens
Productivity	strengthens	weakens
Turnover	strengthens	no change
Absenteeism	little change	little change
Tardiness	no change	little change
Recruiting	strengthens	n.a.
Overtime	no change	no change
Unit labor costs	strengthens	weakens
Utilities costs	no change	little change
What happens to unfavorable effects over time?		
Fatigue	little change	little change
Difficulty of management job	little change	n.a.
Internal communications	no change	n.a.
External communications	no change	n.a.
What happens to mixed effects?		
Coverage	little change	n.a.
Work scheduling	little change	n.a.

Notes: Short-term users had used compressed workweeks for one year or less by 1977, while long-term users had used them for three years or more. Sample sizes are 23 and 79, respectively. The small sample size for short-term users makes the figures for them susceptible to substantial sampling error. There may be differences in the industry, size, or type of compressed workweek used by short-term versus long-term users that could bias these results. The longitudinal comparison utilizes a subset of 21 users in 1977 for whom data were also available from 1974 (Martin, 1975). Because of the small sample size, interpretation of these results must remain tentative. The abbreviation *n.a.* indicates that data were not available to make a longitudinal comparison. See Exhibits 44-A and 44-B for details.

Exhibit 44-A. Key effects of compressed workweeks for short-term and long-term users.

Effect	Short-Term Users	Long-Term Users
Usual or Frequent Good Effects		
(percent reporting better results)		
Employee morale	91	96
Employee commuting	35	62
Productivity	30	48
Absenteeism	65	76
Turnover	52	70
Tardiness	52	53
Recruiting	48	81
Overtime	35	40
Unit labor costs	17	40
Utilities costs	35	40
Occasional Bad Effects		
(percent reporting worse results)		
Fatigue	57	45
Difficulty of management job	22	32
Internal communications	22	27
External communications	27	32
Mixed Effects		
Coverage		
(percent reporting better results)	35	25
(percent reporting worse results)	22	28
Work scheduling		
(percent reporting better results)	35	25
(percent reporting worse results)	17	19

Note: See notes to Exhibit 44.

paring the experiences of long-term users of compressed workweeks (three years or more of use) with the experiences of short-term users (one year or less of use), and by longitudinally comparing the experiences reported by a subset of the 1977 users with the experiences reported by the same users in 1974 for whom data were available (from Martin, 1975). Because the sample sizes for the longitudinal comparison and the short term users in 1977 were small (n=21 and n=23, respectively), the conclusions drawn from this analysis must remain tentative. In addition, short-term and long-term users in 1977 may differ in other characteristics (such as industry, size, and type of compressed workweek used) that could affect their experiences.

Tentative conclusions are that several of the usually favorable effects of compressed workweeks apparently do not change very much if at all over time. Some effects may grow stronger, such as turnover and recruiting benefits (benefits that could only be felt after some time had elapsed) and employee commuting. Trends, for productivity and unit labor costs could not be determined because indications from the two different data sources were in conflict. The occasionally unfavorable effects of compressed workweeks exhibited little or no change over time (see Exhibit 44 for a summary and Exhibits 44-A and 44-B for details).

Another reading of recent versus earlier experiences with compressed workweeks can be ob-

Exhibit 44-B. Longitudinal comparison of key effects of compressed workweeks.

Effects	Percent of Respondents	
	1974	1977
Usual or Frequent Good Effects *(percent reporting better results)*		
Employee commuting	35	67
Productivity	70	35
Turnover	55	60
Absenteeism	75	76
Tardiness	32	45
Overtime	41	33
Unit labor costs	53	30
Utilities costs	32	43
Occasional Bad Effect *(percent reporting worse results)*		
Fatigue	37	45

Note: See notes to Exhibit 44.

tained by comparing the results from this 1977 study with the earlier 1974 survey cited previously and, where possible, with the 1971 AMA survey of the 4-day workweek (Wheeler, Gurman, and Tarnowieski, 1972). These are not longitudinal comparisons because the samples and questionnaires were different, and thus they cannot be used to describe how experiences change with longer duration of use. But when interpreted in light of other information, they may assist in drawing conclusions.

The chief differences between the experiences of the 1977 users in this survey compared with those of the 1974 users were that in the 1977

Exhibit 45. Effects of compressed workweeks on the organization: experiences of the 1977 Nollen and Martin survey and the 1974 Martin survey (percentage of users reporting each effect).

Effects	1974 Survey			1977 Survey		
	Better	No Change	Worse	Better	No Change	Worse
Effects on workers						
Employee commuting	35	58	7	54	34	12
Employee fatigue	7	54	39	9	39	53
Effects on job performance						
Productivity	57	31	12	39	47	14
Turnover	38	62	0	60	38	2
Absenteeism	52	41	7	71	27	2
Tardiness	30	57	13	46	45	9
Effects on costs						
Unit labor cost	27	65	8	36	56	8
Overtime cost	38	45	17	40	49	11
Utilities cost	22	62	16	35	52	12

Notes: Sample sizes are n=66 for the 1974 survey and n=148 for the 1977 survey. Because the 1974 and 1977 surveys differ somewhat in the industrial and size distribution of their respondents, comparisons about changes over time cannot be made. See Exhibits 44 and 46.

Exhibit 46. Characteristics of the 1974 Martin sample of compressed workweek users compared with 1977 Nollen and Martin sample.

Characteristic	1974 Sample (percent)	1977 Sample (percent)
Industry		
Manufacturing	47	38
Transportation, communications, utilities	4	4
Wholesale and retail trade	2	5
Finance, insurance, real estate	14	22
Services	20	8
Government	2	4
Diversified and other	12	18
Sector		
Private	83	92
(profit)	(74)	(85)
(nonprofit)	(9)	(7)
Public	17	8
Number of Employees		
Less than 100	22	11
100 to 499	44	30
500 to 1000	17	11
More than 1000	17	48
Duration of Use		
Less than six months	9	11
Six months to one year	6	9
One to two years	21	7
Two to three years	9	16
More than three years	56	57

Note: Sample sizes are n=66 for 1974, n=148 for 1977.

survey (1) productivity improvements were noted less often and fatigue may have been a problem more often and (2) turnover, absenteeism, and tardiness were improved more often. Effects on costs were not significantly different. The adverse developments in both productivity and fatigue may be traceable to the smaller proportion of manufacturing firms and small firms in the 1977 survey (previous results suggested that these firms may have better experiences with productivity and fatigue than do other firms—see Exhibits 45 and 46). The productivity experiences of compressed workweeks users in the 1971 survey were superior to those in the 1977 survey—66 percent reported better productivity versus the 39 percent figure for 1977.

The outcome of these very rough investigations into whether users' experiences with compressed workweeks change over time is that there is no strong evidence that they do. With the possible exceptions of productivity and perhaps fatigue, there seems to be little or no reason for discontinuing compressed workweeks on the basis of a weakening of experiences.

Experiences of Discontinuers

The experiences reported by organizations that dropped compressed workweeks are generally less favorable than the experiences reported by continuing users. But are there any areas in which especially bad experiences trigger discontinuation? How do the experiences of discontinuers compare with the expectations of organizations that have never used compressed workweeks and do not plan to use them?

The widest divergences in the experiences of discontinuers compared with those of continuing successful users occur for productivity and unit labor costs. They were frequently negative experiences for discontinuers (nearly half the time) whereas for continuing users they were frequently positive experiences. Other wide divergences occurred for fatigue and the difficulty of the management job, which were worsened for most discontinuers (as opposed to half or less of continuing users). Coverage of work situations, work scheduling, and relationships with customers were problems for half the discontinuers. For them, improvement in tardiness ceased to be an advantage of compressed workweeks. There were also some failures that may have been prompted by bad overtime experiences (see Exhibit 47 and compare with Exhibit 27).

Several effects of compressed workweeks were not much different in the cases of failures than in the cases of successful uses. They are turnover, absenteeism, recruiting, communications,

utilities costs, employee commuting, and relationships with suppliers. None of these can be explanations for failures.

With some exceptions, the experiences of discontinuers were very much like the expectations of organizations that have never used compressed workweeks and do not plan to do so (compare Exhibit 47 with Exhibit 33). If these non-users are well-informed, this result suggests that perhaps the original adoption of compressed workweeks by eventual discontinuers was a mistake—that the work setting was not suited to successful use of this work schedule.

Reasons for Discontinuing Compressed Workweeks

The major reason reported by organizations that discontinued their use of compressed workweeks is a complex of scheduling, supervision, coverage, and/or customer service problems—nearly half of all discontinuers cited one or more of these reasons. Ranking second as reasons for failure were bad productivity experiences (19 percent) and high operating costs (15 percent, plus 6 percent who specified overtime

Exhibit 47. Experiences of organizations that discontinued compressed workweeks.

Effect	Change Attributed to Compressed Workweeks (percent of all discontinuers)		
	Better	No Change	Worse
Effects that were bad and much different than for continuing users			
Productivity	19	37	44
Fatigue	5	12	82
Difficulty of management job	7	25	70
Coverage of work situations	16	30	54
Work scheduling	14	36	50
Unit labor costs	13	46	40
Relationship with customers	12	40	47
Effects that were not as positive as they were for continuing users			
Tardiness	21	57	23
Overtime costs	28	37	35
Employee morale	65	21	14

Notes: The sample size is n=58. See Exhibits 27 and 33 for comparison with experiences of continuing users and expectations of non-users.

Exhibit 48. Reasons given by organizations that discontinued compressed workweeks.

Reason	Percent of All Discontinuers
Internal work scheduling, supervision, communication, or provision of facilities made too difficult	27
Customer relations, customer service, or coverage made too difficult	19
Productivity decreased	19
Employees did not like it, usually due to conflict with personal schedules or commuting	17
Operating costs (not otherwise specified) increased	15
Fatigue	11
Overtime costs too high	6
Top management opposed it (reasons not specified)	6
Used for special reason or temporary need that is no longer present	19
Other	4

Notes: Totals exceed 100 percent because of multiple responses. The sample size is 68 responses from 48 discontinuers.

costs in particular). Also in the second rank were quite a few cases of employee dissatisfaction (17 percent), usually stemming from conflicts with home and family schedules. Fatigue was less often mentioned as a reason for failure (see Exhibit 48). A substantial number of discontinuers dropped the compressed workweek because it was instituted for a special purpose or temporary use in the first place. In these cases, compressed workweeks did not really fail to produce the results desired; rather, the need for them passed.

These reasons for dropping compressed workweeks support the notion that there are certain work situations for which they are suited and others for which they should not be used. The only effect of compressed workweeks on the organization that appears not to yield what is expected of it with any frequency is productivity; this is the only experience users have that turns out negatively—perhaps weakening beyond tolerable limits or showing up only after some duration of use. Otherwise, failures appear to be a matter of a mismatch between the work setting and the compressed workweek.

Will the Use of Compressed Workweeks Increase in the Future?

A variety of findings from this survey and others suggest that the use of compressed workweeks is limited to special purposes and that its growth, if there is to be any at all, will be very small. Here is the evidence, in terms of raw statistics:

- The U.S. Bureau of Labor Statistics reports that the number of workers on compressed workweeks in 1976 declined slightly from the figure in 1975, following several years of rapid growth. (Some of this growth was for a temporary reason, such as a response to the energy crisis of 1974.) From this survey, few of the 1977 users of compressed workweeks (27 percent) had instituted it in the last two years (since 1975). Instead, most users had started it more than two years ago.
- Scarcely any organizations (only 2 percent) are currently planning or evaluating its use. By contrast, 16 percent have formally considered compressed workweeks but rejected their use.

- Failures of compressed workweeks occur surprisingly often. The failure rate in this sample was 28 percent, which is somewhat higher than previous estimates.

A review of the experiences that users, discontinuers, and non-users have with the compressed workweek indicates that it is likely to be successful in some work settings but not others, and hence of limited growth potential. For example, compressed workweeks are usually found in only some, but not all, work units in a user organization. The experiences of organizations that drop compressed workweeks because of bad effects on the organization are very different from the experiences reported by continuing users, but quite similar to the expectations of non-users—organizations that have never used compressed workweeks and do not plan to adopt them. The usual reasons for dropping compressed workweeks are work technology reasons. It is usually not a matter of deterioration of results from compressed workweeks over time. Many organizations that considered but then decided against using compressed workweeks also said incompatibility with their operations was the reason.

All these findings indicate that there are suitable and unsuitable work settings for compressed workweeks, and that widespread use should not be anticipated. Growth in compressed workweeks will depend on how many suitable places there are for it, and this is not well known.

One policy change could remove the overtime payments constraint on the use of compressed workweeks. (Such payments were the barrier cited by a substantial number of organizations that once considered but then decided against using them). If the provisions (in both federal labor law and labor union contracts) that require overtime pay for hours worked beyond eight in a day were modified to hours worked beyond 40 in a week, new opportunities for the use of compressed workweeks would open up.

Bibliography

1. Bureau of National Affairs, *ASPA-BNA Survey: The Changing Workweek* (Washington, D.C.: Bureau of National Affairs, January 6, 1972)

2. Davis, Richard, A Cross-Sectional Study of the Impact of the Transition to the Four-Day Work Week on Employee Job Satisfaction," unpublished Ph.D. dissertation, Florida State University, 1973.

3. Dobelis, M.C., "The Three-day Week—Offshoot of an EDP Operation," *Personnel*, January-February 1972.

4. Dworaczek, Marian, and Matthews, Catherine J., *Recent Innovations in Work Scheduling: A Bibliography* (Toronto: Ontario Ministry of Labor Research Library, 1974).

5. Glickman, Albert S., and Brown, Xenia, *Changing Schedules of Work: Patterns and Implications* (Kalamazoo: W.E. Upjohn Institute for Employment Research, 1974).

6. Goodale, James G., and Aagaard, A.K., "Factors Relating to Varying Reactions to the 4-Day Workweek," *Journal of Applied Psychology*, February 1975.

7. Greiner, John M., "Employee Incentives in Local Government: Repackaging Working Hours," *Labor-Management Relations Service Newsletter*, August 1973.

8. Greiner, John M.; Bell, Lynn; and Hatry, Harry P., *Employee Incentives to Improve State and Local Government* (Washington, D.C.: National Commission on Productivity and Quality of Working Life, 1975).

9. Haldi Associates, Inc., *Alternative Work Schedules: A Technology Assessment* (Washington, D.C.: National Science Foundation, ASRA Information Resources Center, 1977).

10. Hartman, Richard; Weaver, A.; and Marit, K., "Four Factors Influencing Conversion to a Four-day Workweek," *Human Resource Management,* Spring 1977.

11. Hawk, D.L., and Dunham, R.B., *The Four-day/ Forty-hour Workweek: A Selected Bibliography,* Exchange Bibliography No. 1248 (Monticello, Illinois: Council of Planning Librarians, 1977).

12. Hedges, Janice N., "A Look at the 4-day Workweek," *Monthly Labor Review,* October 1971.

13. _____, "How Many Days Make a Workweek?" *Monthly Labor Review,* April 1975.

14. _____, "New Patterns for Working Time," *Monthly Labor Review,* February 1973.

15. Hellriegel, Don, "The 4-day Workweek: A Review and Assessment," *Business Topics,* Spring 1972.

16. Ivancevich, John M., "Effects of the Shorter Workweek on Selected Satisfaction and Performance Measures," *Journal of Applied Psychology,* December 1974.

17. Jaffe, A.; Friedman, N.; and Rogers, T., Rearranged *Work Schedules in the Private Sector* (New York: Columbia University Bureau of Applied Social Research, forthcoming).

18. Martin, Virginia H., *Hours of Work When Workers Can Choose: The Experience of 59 Organizations with Employee-Chosen Staggered Hours and Flexitime* (Washington, D.C.: Business and Professional Women's Foundation, 1975).

19. Mathis, Robert L., "The Immediate Effects of a Conversion to the Four-day Workweek on the Overall Job Satisfaction of Selected Nursing Service Personnel," dissertation, University of Colorado, 1972.

20. Nollen, Stanley D.; Eddy, Brenda B.; and Martin Virginia H., *Part-time Employment: The Manager's Perspective* (New York: Praeger Publishers, Inc., 1978).

21. Nollen, Stanley D. and Martin, Virginia H., *Alternative Work Schedules, Part I: Flexitime* (New York: AMACOM, a division of American Management Associations, 1978).

22. Nord, W.R., and Costigan, R., "Worker Adjustment to the Four-day Week: A Longitudinal Study," *Journal of Applied Psychology,* August 1973.

23. Poor, Riva, *4 Days, 40 Hours* (Cambridge: Bursk and Poor Publishing, Inc., 1970).

24. Society for Humanistic Management, Conference on Human Productivity and the Rearranged Workweek, November 1972, Report in *Journal for Humanistic Management,* Vol. 1, No. 1, 1973.

25. Steele, James Lee, "An Investigation of Work and Leisure Experiences of Workers in Two Assembly Plants in Rural Settings," unpublished Ph.D. dissertation, University of Montana, 1974.

26. Swerdloff, Sol, *The Revised Workweek: Results of a Pilot Study of 16 Firms,* Bulletin 1846 (Washington, D.C.: U.S. Department of Labor, Bureau of Labor Statistics, 1975).

27. Swierczewski, Thomas J., "A Study of One Firm's Installation and Utilization of a 4-day Week," thesis, City University of New York, 1972.

28. Tellier, Richard D., "The Four-day Workweek and the Elderly: A Cross-sectional Study," *Journal of Gerontology,* July 1974.

29. U.S. Comptroller General, *Legal Limitations on Flexible and Compressed Work Schedules for Federal Employees,* Report to the Congress (Washington, D.C.: U.S. General Accounting Office, 1974).

30. U.S. Comptroller General, *Contractors' Use of Altered Work Schedules for Their Employees—How Is It Working?* Report to the Congress (Washington, D.C.: U.S. General Accounting Office, 1976).

31. U.S. Department of Labor Library, *The Shorter Workweek and Flexible Hours: A Bibliography* No. 1974-0-549-634 (Washington, D.C.: U.S. Government Printing Office, 1974).

32. Weinstein, Harriet G., "A Comparison of Three Alternative Work Schedules: Flexible Work Hours, Compact Work Week, and Staggered Work Hours," dissertation, Industrial Research Unit, The Wharton School, University of Pennsylvania, 1975.

33. Wheeler, Kenneth E.; Gurman, Richard; and Tarnowieski, Dale, *The Four-Day Week* (New York: AMACOM, a division of American Management Associations, 1972).

34. Wilson, James A., ed., *The Four-day Workweek: Fad or Future?* Proceedings of a Conference, June 17, 1972 (Pittsburgh: University of Pittsburgh, 1973).

5 871